Hamilton Ontario Book 5 in Colour Photos, Saving Our History One Photo at a Time

Photography
by Barbara Raué
2014

Series Name:
Cruising Ontario

Book 91 – Hamilton Book 5

Cover photo: 46 Herkimer Street

Series Name: Cruising Ontario
Saving Our History One Photo at a Time
in colour photos

Book 33: Southampton
Book 34: Jarvis
Book 35: Hagersville
Book 36: Caledonia
Book 37: Simcoe
Book 38-41: Cambridge
Book 42-43: Kitchener
Book 46: Shelburne
Book 47: Alton, Mono
Book 48: London Colour
Book 49: St. Thomas
Book 50-52: Orangeville
Book 53-55: Dundas
Book 56: Stratford
Book 57: Hanover
Book 58-59: New Hamburg
Book 60: Waterdown
Book 61: Burlington
Book 62: Stoney Creek
Book 63: Seaforth
Book 64: Aberfoyle,
Morriston and Rockton
Book 65: Eden Mills
Book 66: Ancaster and
Mount Hope
Book 67: Jarvis,Pt.Dover
Book 68-69: Fergus, Elora
Book 70-71: Elmira
Book72:St.Jacobs, St.Clements,
Heidelberg,Crosshill,Bamberg

Book 73: Linwood, Macton
Book 74: Wellesley
Book 75: Listowel
Book 76: Palmerston
Book 77:Dorchester to Aylmer
Book 78-79: Aylmer
Book 80: Drayton & Area
Book 81: Tillsonburg
Book 82: Arthur
Book 83: Rockwood
Book 84: Acton
Book 85-86: Guelph
Book 87-91: Hamilton
Book 92-93: Owen Sound

Other Books by Barbara Raue

Coins of Gold

Arrows, Indians and Love

The Life and Times of Barbara
Volume 1: Inventions That Have Enhanced My Life
Volume 2: Entertainment That I Have Enjoyed
Volume 3: East Coast Trips
Volume 4: Olympics Have Always Intrigued Me
Volume 5: Wonders of the World
Volume 6: Caribbean Cruises We Have Enjoyed
Volume 7: Animals
Volume 8: Storms and Other Major Disasters in My Lifetime
Volume 9: Wars, Terrorist Attacks and Major Disasters

The Cromwell Family Book

Laura Secord Discovered

Visit Barbara's website to view all of her books
http://barbararaue.ca

John Ryckman, born in Barton township (where present day downtown Hamilton is), described the area in 1803 as he remembered it: "The city in 1803 was all forest. The shores of the bay were difficult to reach or see because they were hidden by a thick, almost impenetrable mass of trees and undergrowth... Bears ate pigs, so settlers warred on bears. Wolves gobbled sheep and geese, so they hunted and trapped wolves. They also held organized raids on rattlesnakes on the mountainside. There was plenty of game. Many a time have I seen a deer jump the fence into my back yard, and there were millions of pigeons which we clubbed as they flew low."

Hamilton, the centre of a densely populated and industrialized region, is located in Southern Ontario on the western part of Lake Ontario. Hamilton Harbour marks the northern limit of the city, and the Niagara Escarpment runs through the middle of the city bisecting it into "upper" and "lower" parts. There are over one hundred waterfalls and cascades within the city, most of which are on or near the Bruce Trail as it winds through the Niagara Escarpment.

Two steel manufacturing companies, Stelco and Dofasco, were formed in 1910 and 1912, and Procter & Gamble opened a manufacturing plant in 1914. McMaster University moved from Toronto to Hamilton, an airport was built in 1940, a Studebaker assembly line started in 1948, the Burlington Bay Skyway Bridge was built in 1958, and the first Tim Horton's store opened in 1964.

On January 1, 2001, the new City of Hamilton was formed through the amalgamation of the former city and the six municipalities of Stoney Creek, Glanbrook, Ancaster, Dundas, and Flamborough. We have lived in Hamilton for more than 40 years; it is here that we raised our three children.

Table of Contents

Kent Street   Page 6

Herkimer Street   Page 7

James Street South   Page 17

MacNab Street South   Page 24

Queen Street South   Page 30

Forest Avenue   Page 45

Hess Street South   Page 47
    206 Main Street West at Hess   Page 50

Park Street South   Page 51

Park Street North   Page 51

Catharine Street North   Page 53

King Street West   Page 54

Architectural Terms   Page 55

Building Styles   Page 58

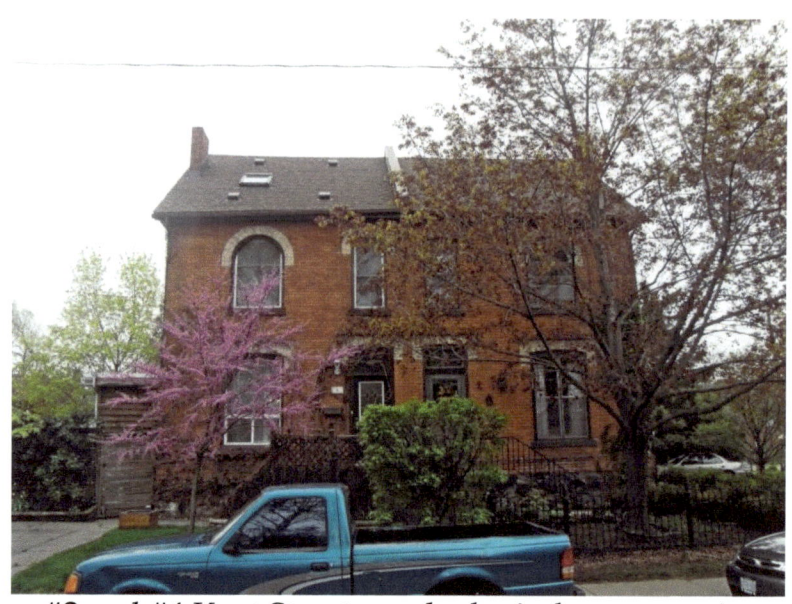

#2 and #4 Kent Street – arched window voussoirs

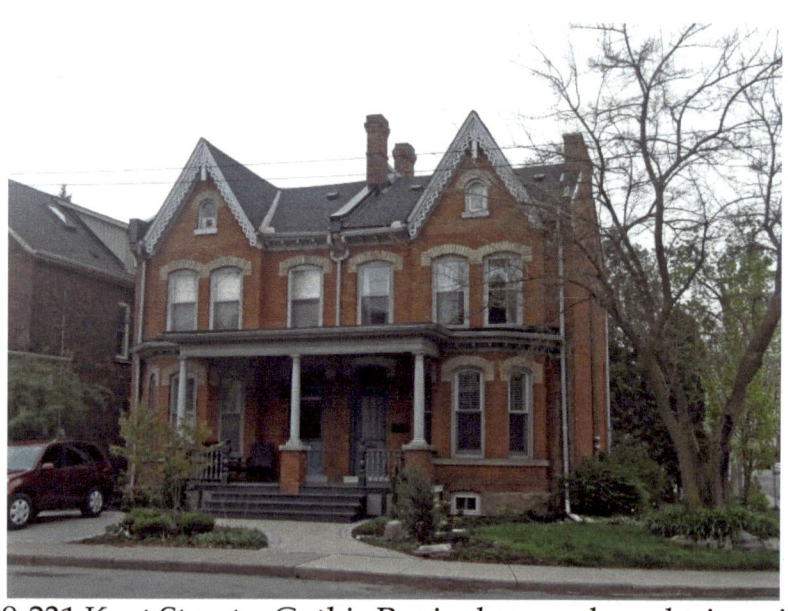

229-231 Kent Street – Gothic Revival, verge board trim with finials on gables, arched window voussoirs

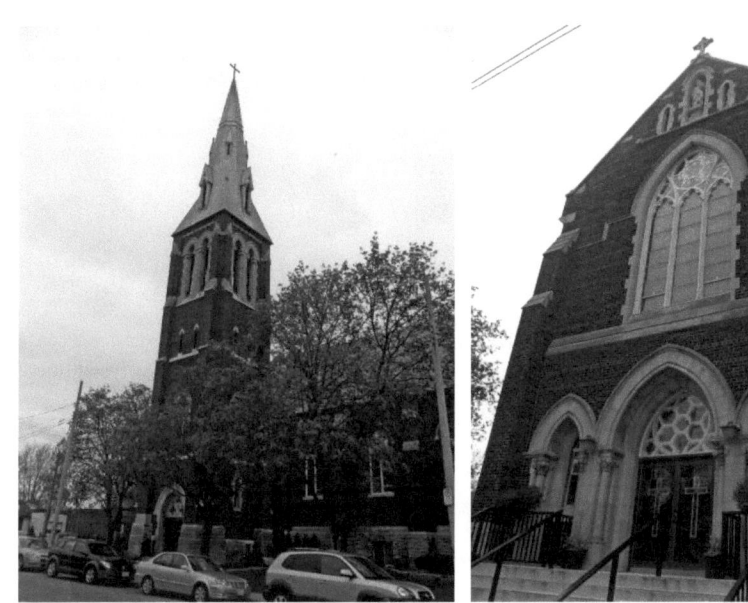

260 Herkimer Street – St. Joseph's Roman Catholic Church
Rose window, buttresses

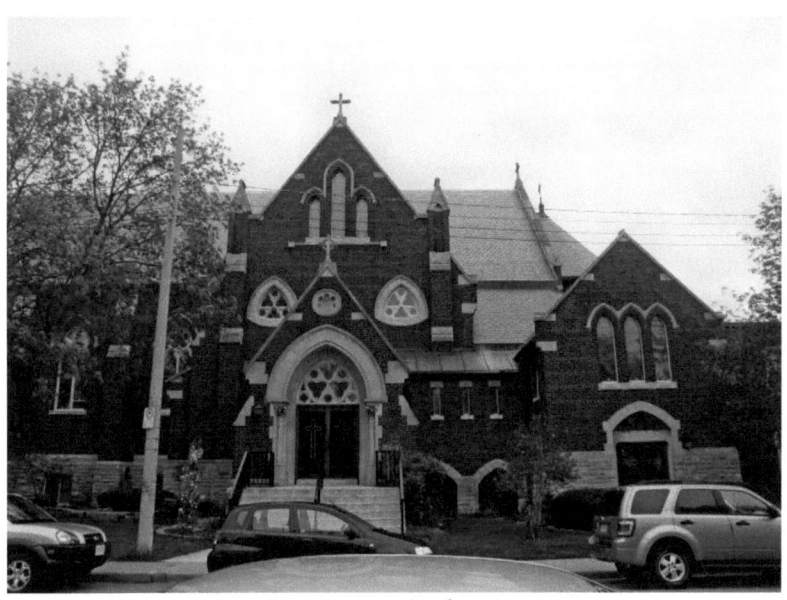

Lancet windows

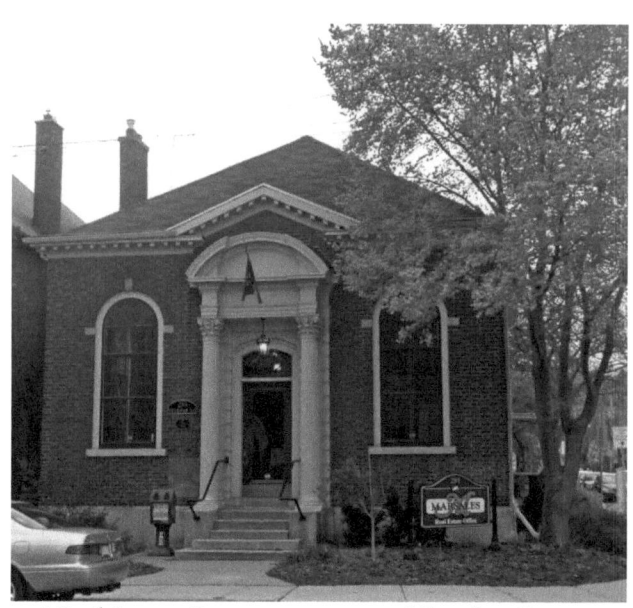

Herkimer Street, corner of Locke Street

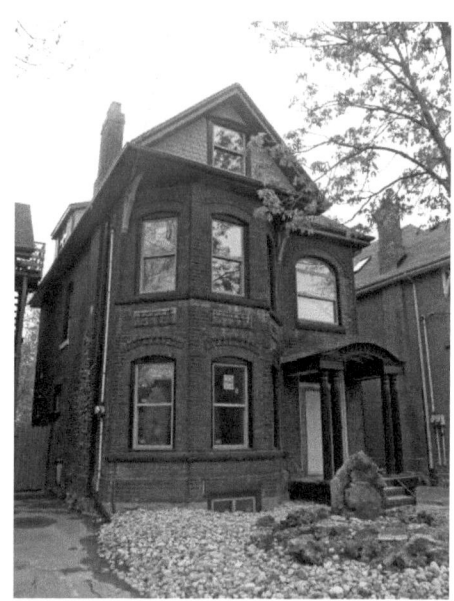

220 Herkimer Street, where we lived on the ground floor
from 1973-1975; Edwardian; two-storey bay window

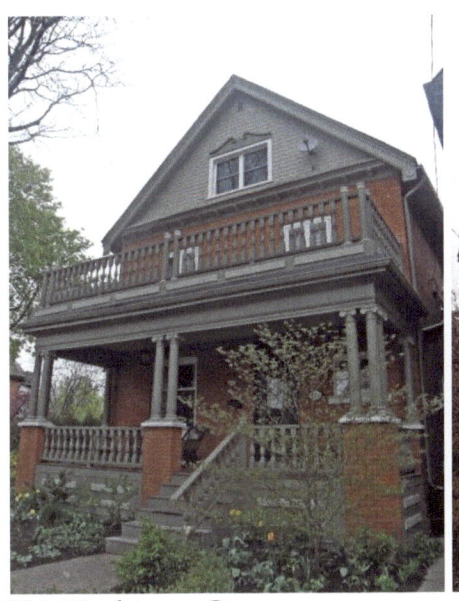

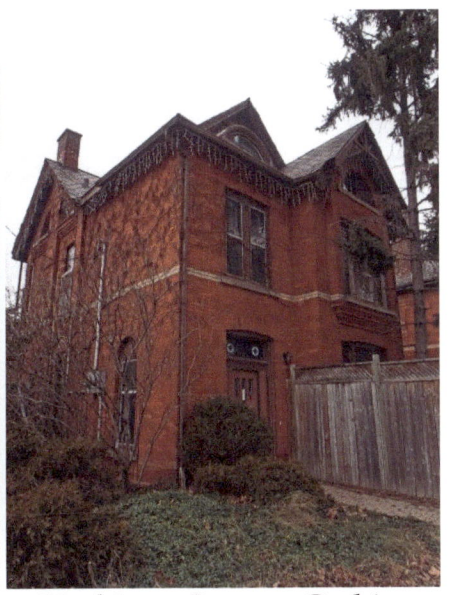

221 Herkimer Street
Edwardian, balcony 2nd floor
Ionic capitals on pillars

Herkimer Street – Gothic

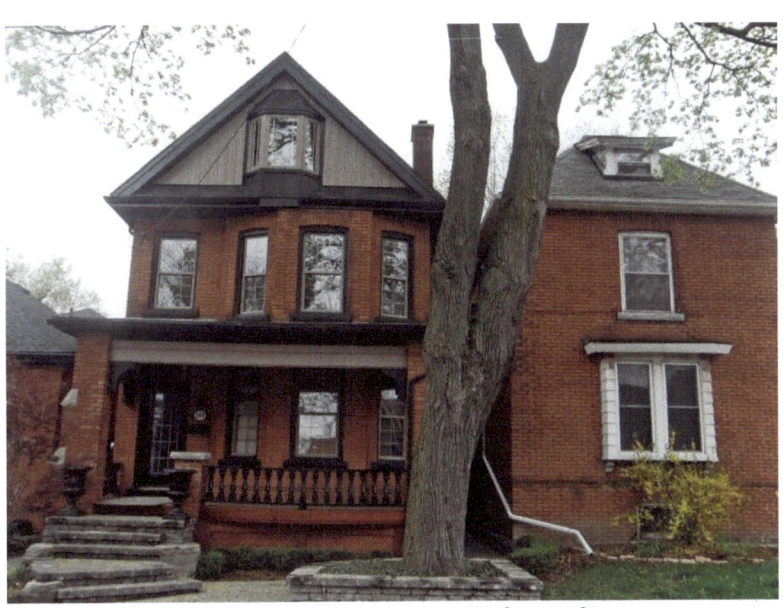

249 Herkimer Street – Edwardian

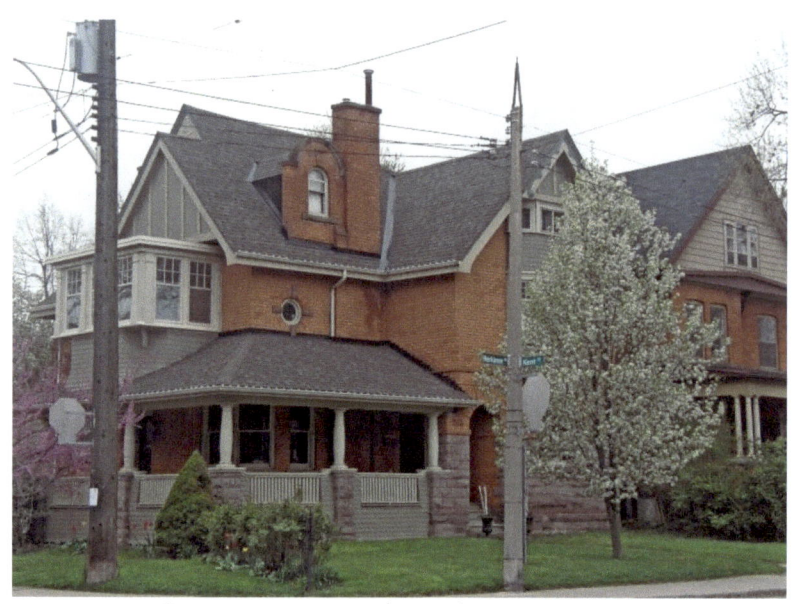

Corner Kent and Herkimer Streets

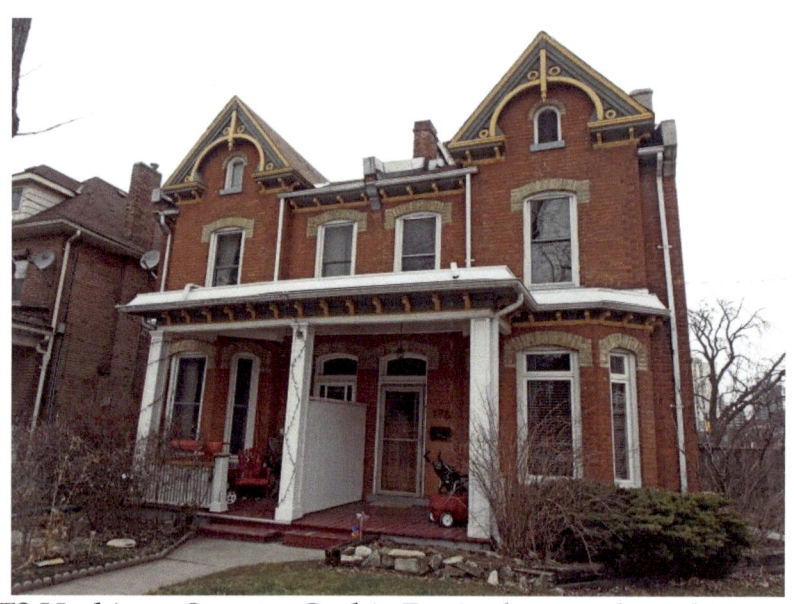

178 Herkimer Street – Gothic Revival, verge board trim on gables, cornice brackets, bay windows

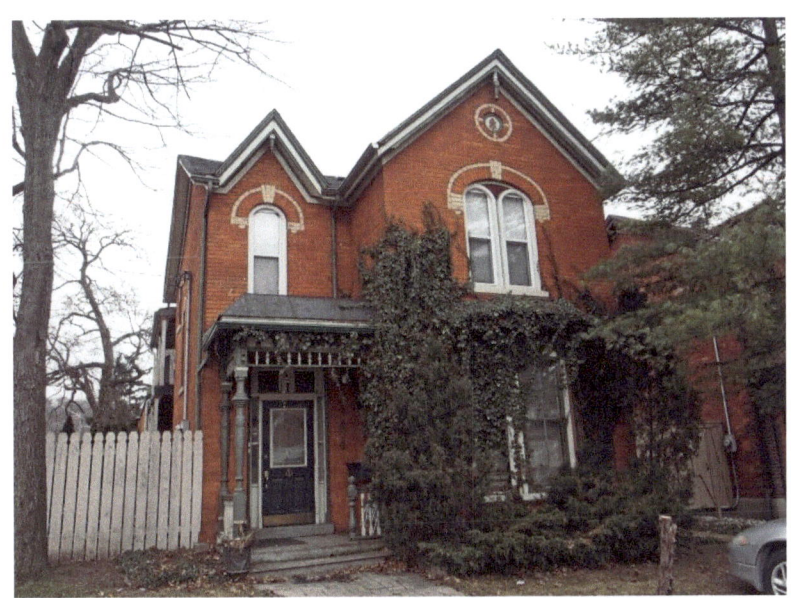

181 Herkimer Street – Gothic Revival

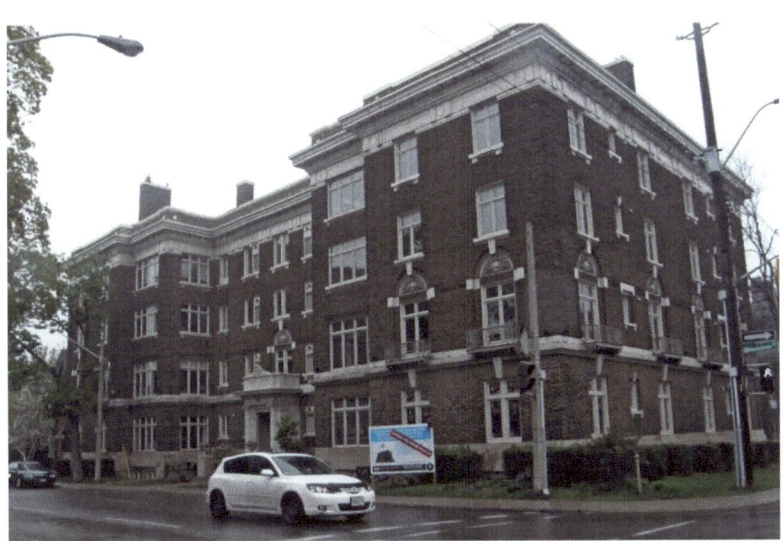

86 Herkimer Street – Herkimer Apartments

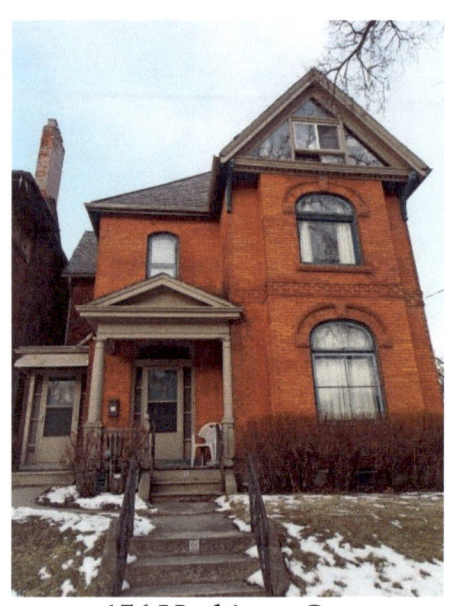

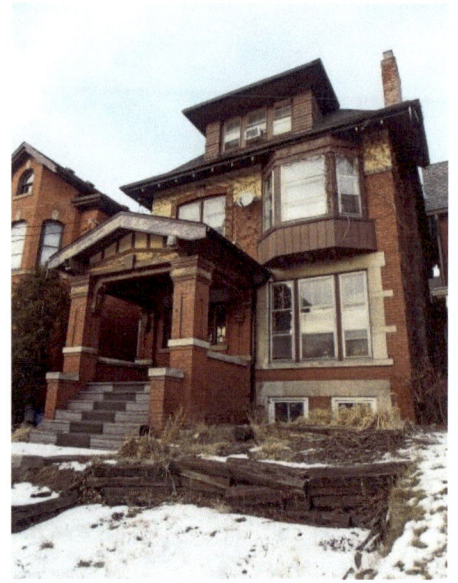

156 Herkimer Street
Edwardian, pediment

158 Herkimer Street
Italianate, dormer

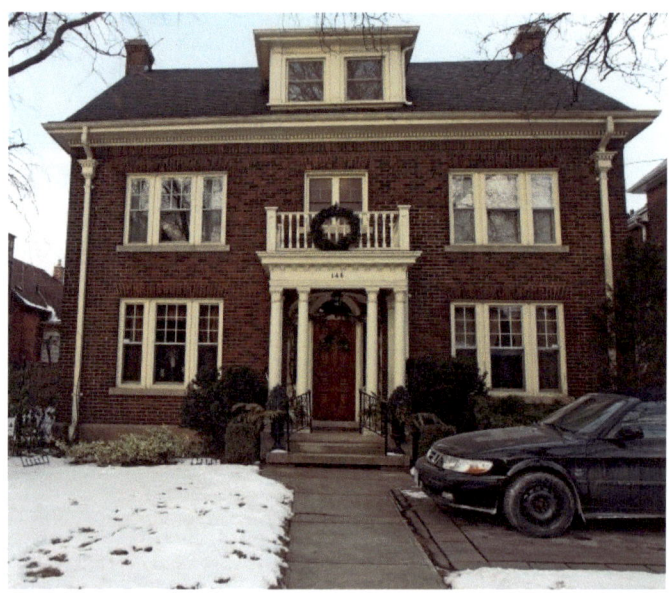

146 Herkimer – Georgian, balcony, dormer

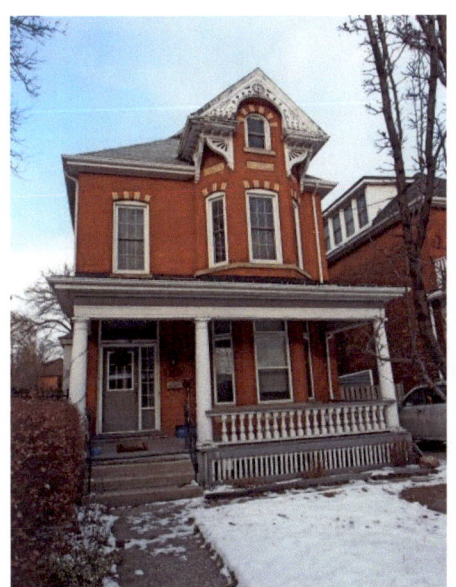 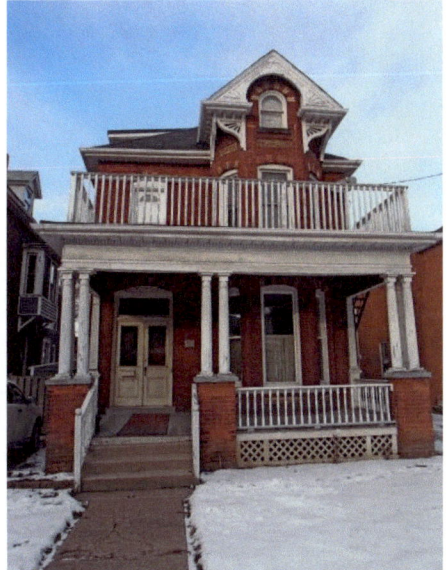

144 Herkimer Street   142 Herkimer Street

Fretwork, verge board trim on gable

Full-width 2nd floor balcony

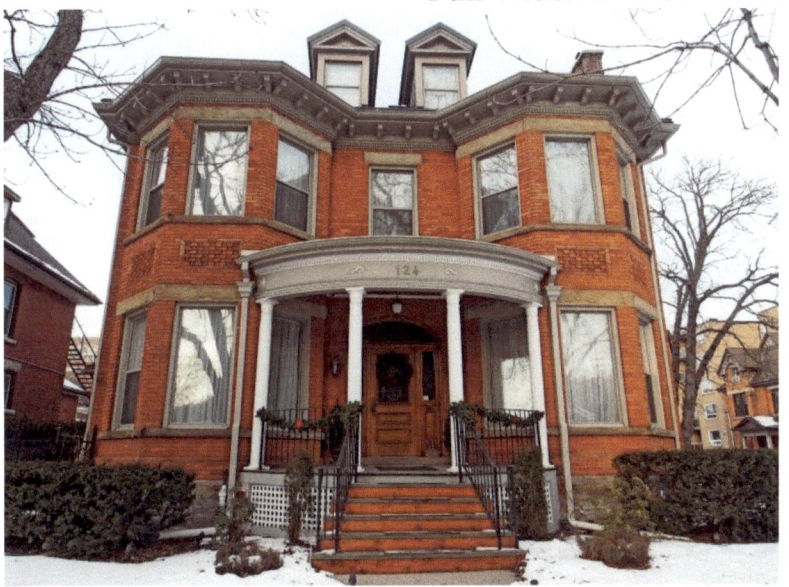

124 Herkimer Street – Neo-Classical, two-storey bays, cornice brackets, dormers

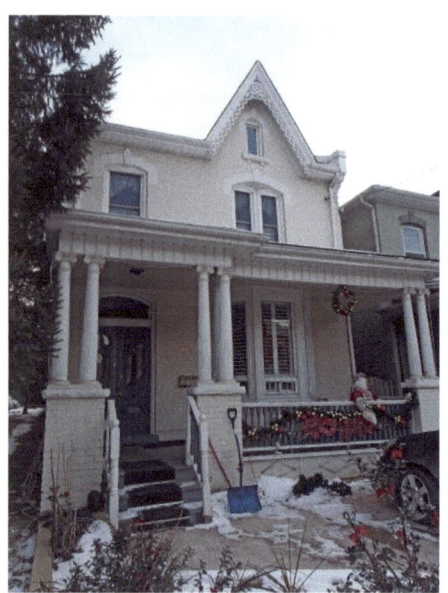

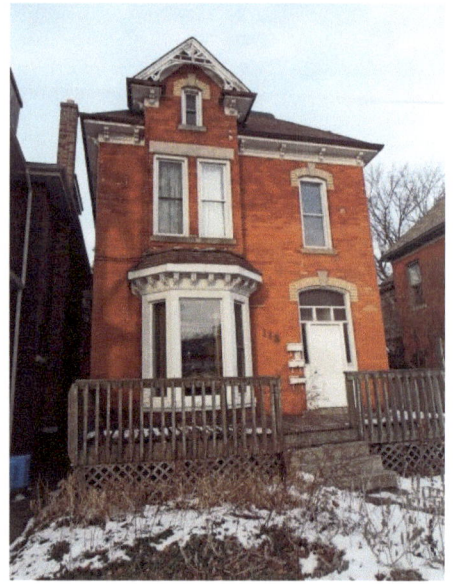

141 Herkimer Street
Gothic Revival, Ionic capitals
verge board trim on gable

118 Herkimer Street
bay window,
cornice brackets

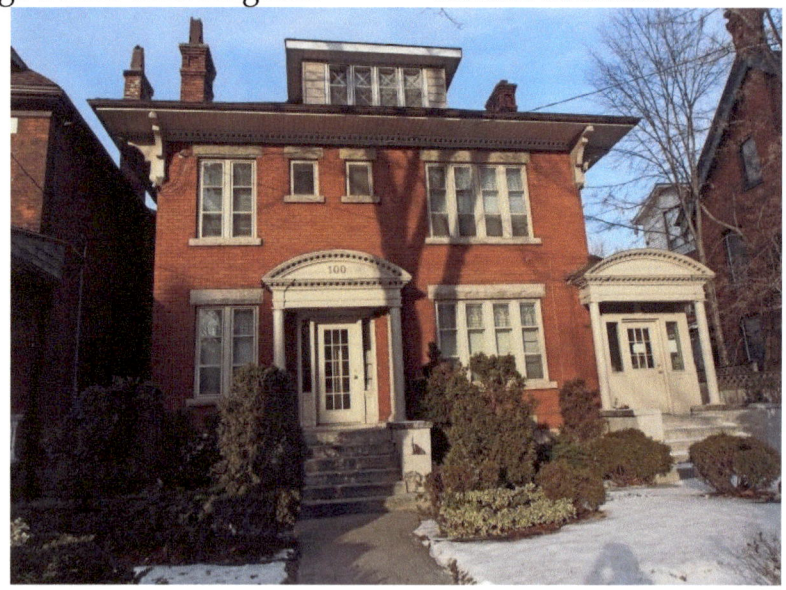

100 Herkimer Street – Neo-Classical, dormer

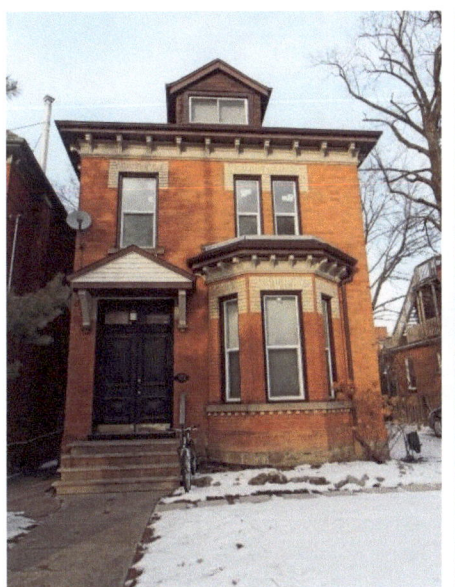

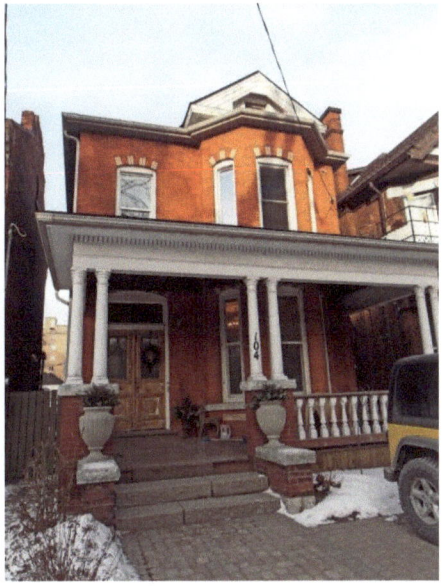

112 Herkimer Street
Italianate, cornice brackets
Bay window, pediment

104 Herkimer Street
Italianate
dichromatic brickwork

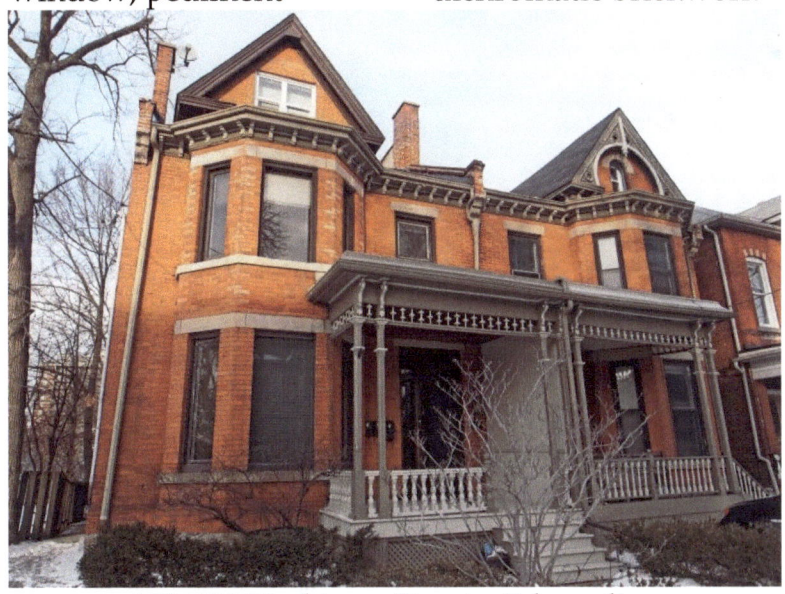

108-106 Herkimer Street - Edwardian

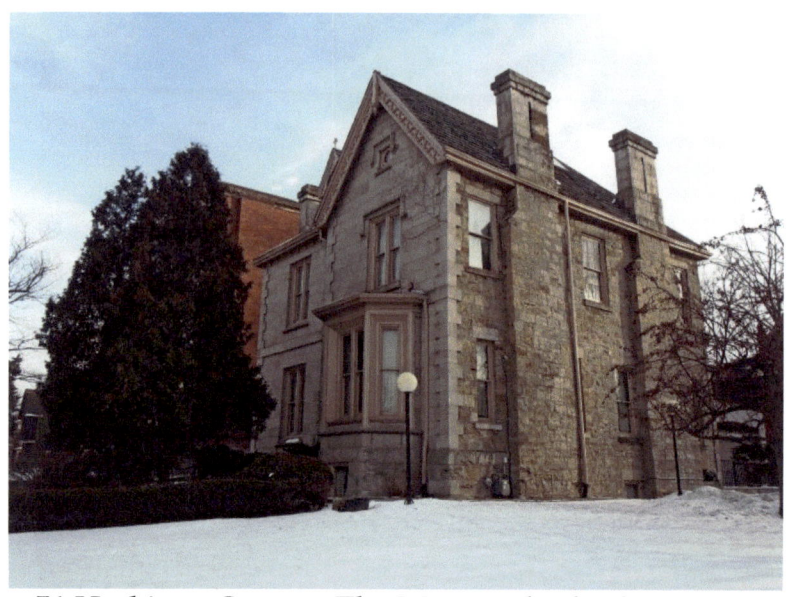

51 Herkimer Street – The Manse – built 1858, stone

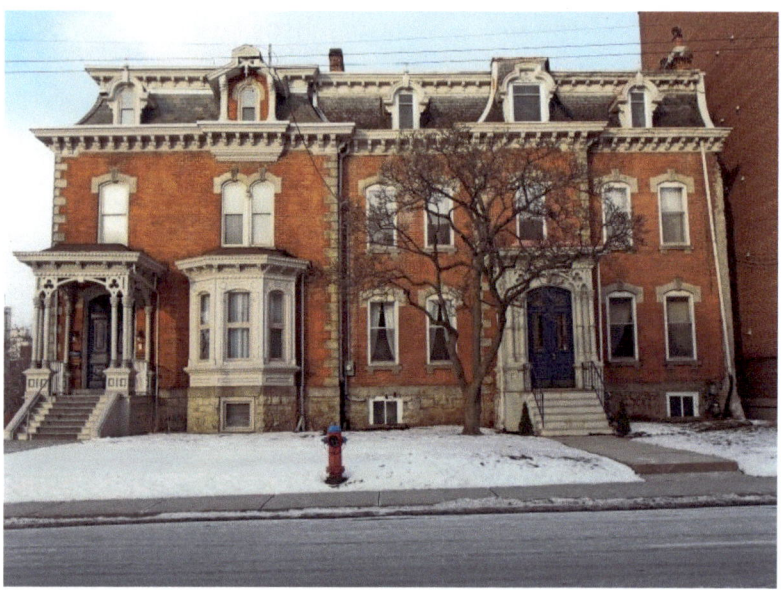

46 Herkimer Street – Second Empire, mansard roof, dormers with decorative window hoods, entrance ways, bay windows, corner quoins, cornice brackets

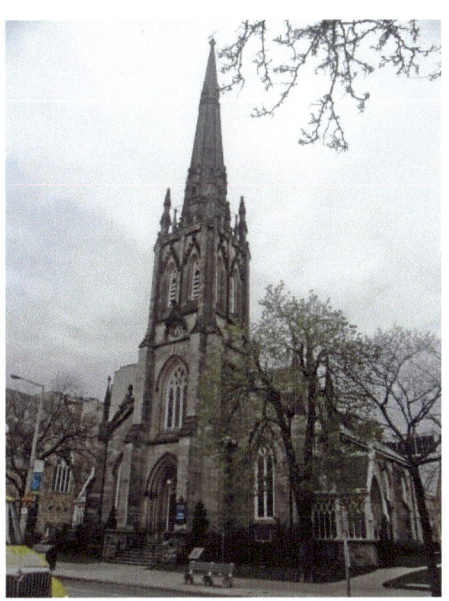

70 James Street South - St. Paul's Presbyterian Church
Begun in 1854 and completed 3 years later, it was designed in the Gothic Revival style. The elegant 80 foot spire set atop a hundred foot tower marks the building as an outstanding example of Canadian Victorian church architecture.

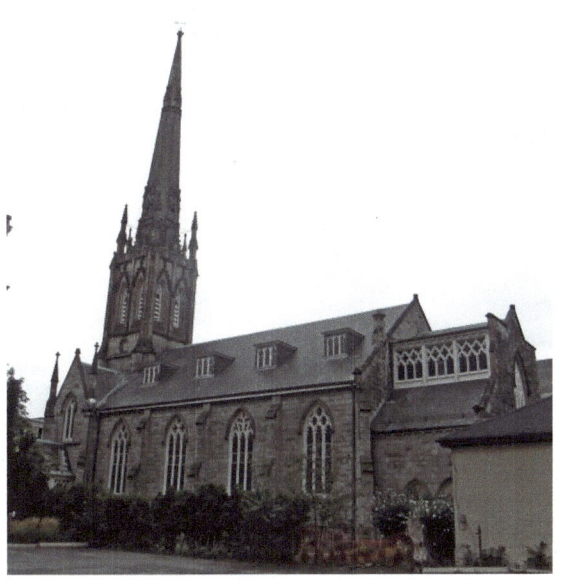

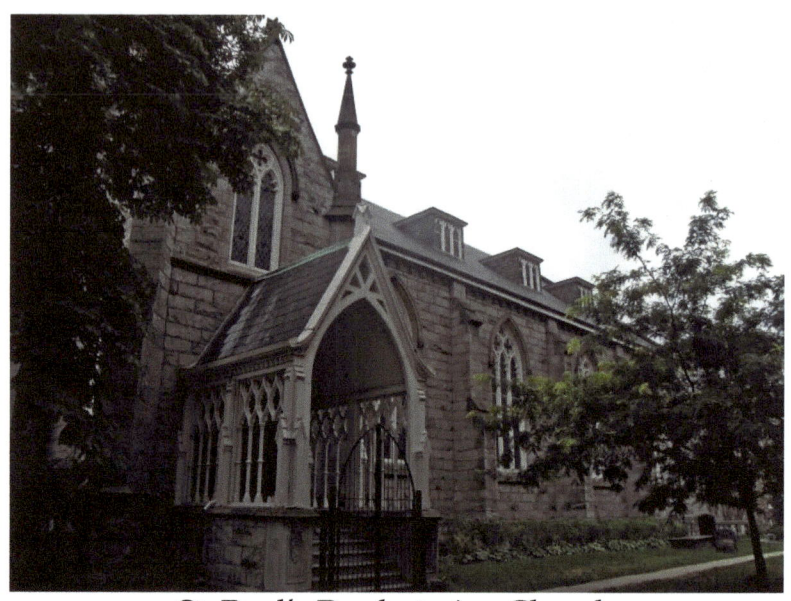

St. Paul's Presbyterian Church

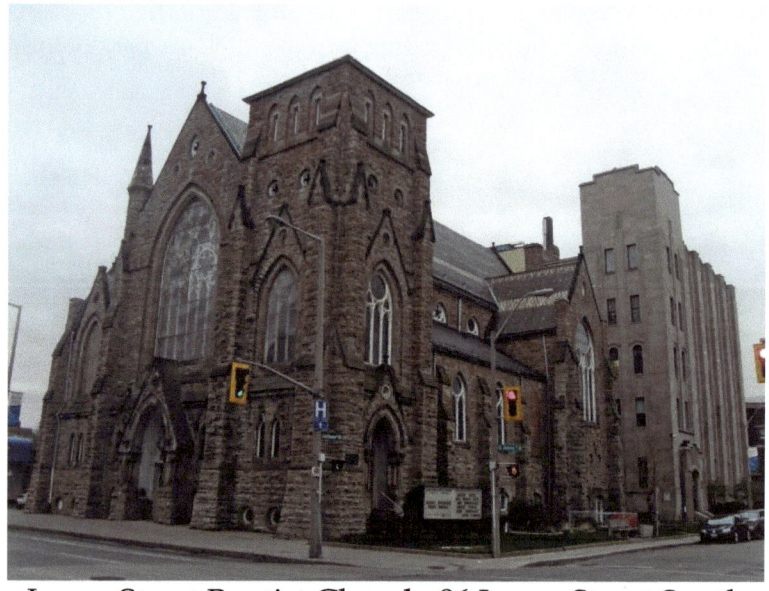

James Street Baptist Church, 96 James Street South
Built 1878-82 in the Gothic style with pointed arches, slim
pillars and stained glass windows

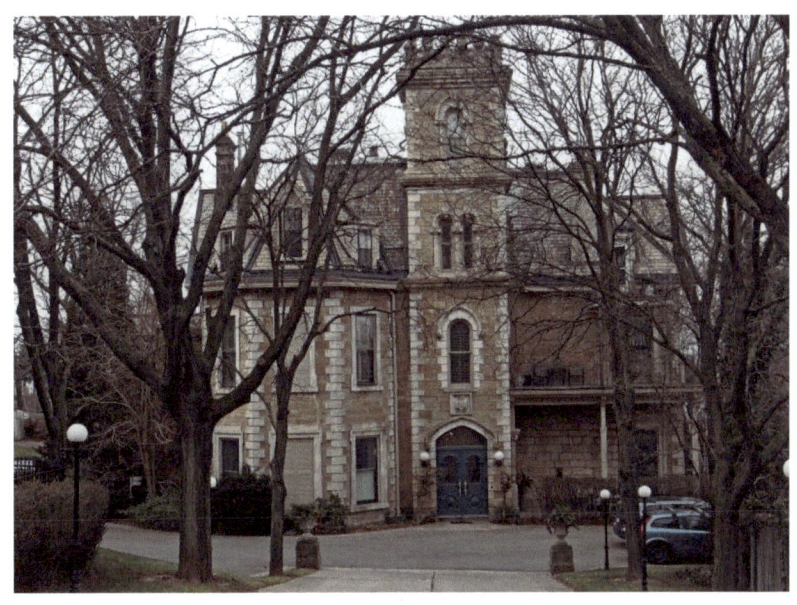

316 James Street South – Ballinahinch – stone architecture
1850, corner quoins, crenelated tower,
decorative window hoods and keystones

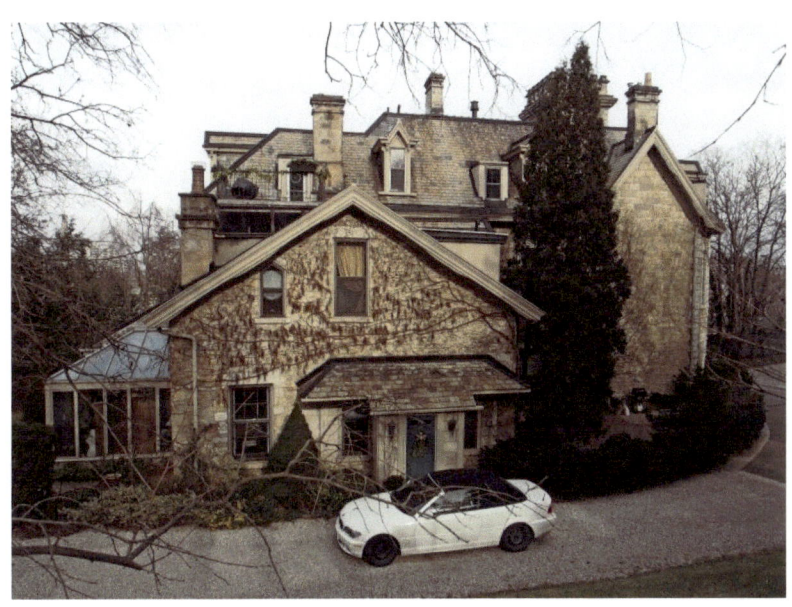

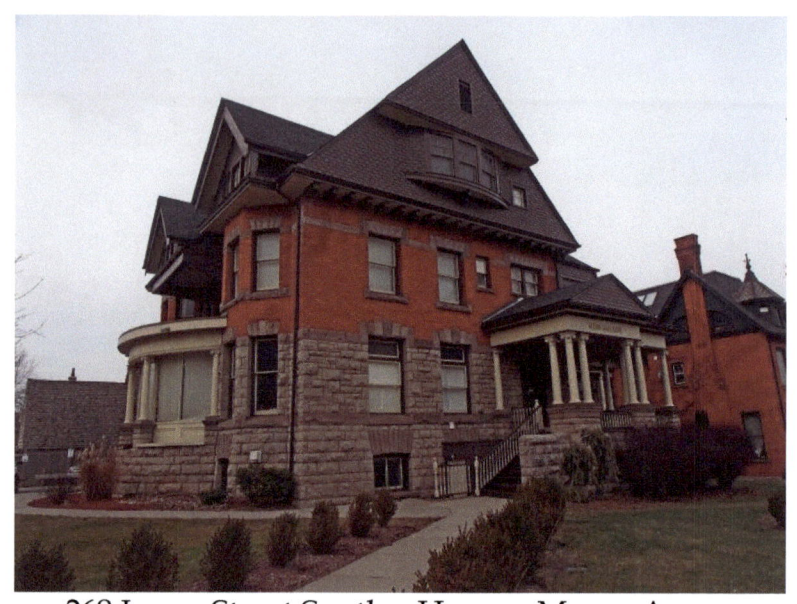

268 James Street South – Henson Manor Annex

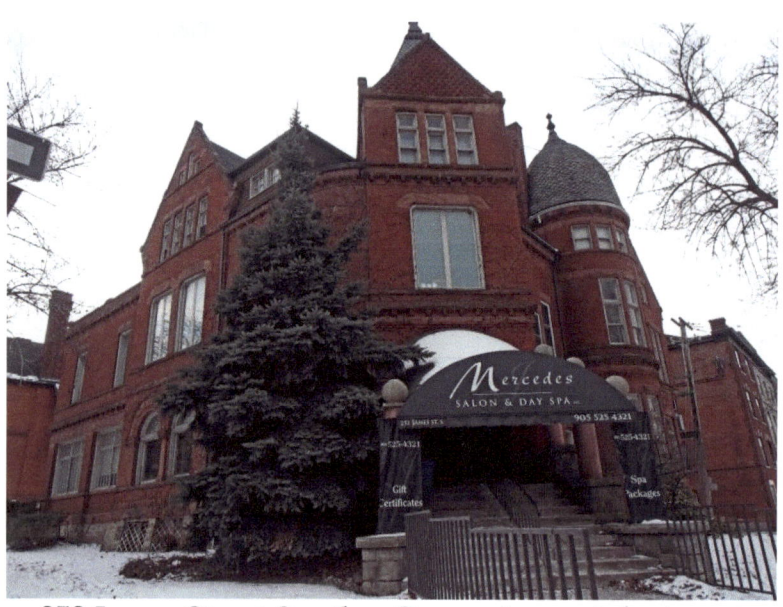

252 James Street South – Queen Anne style, turret

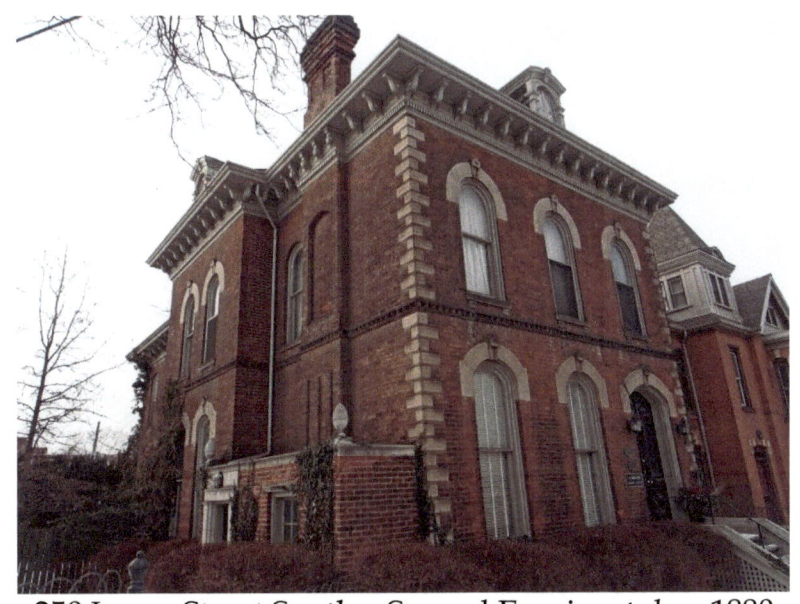

250 James Street South – Second Empire style – 1880
Cornice brackets, dormers, corner quoins, arched window
voussoirs with keystones

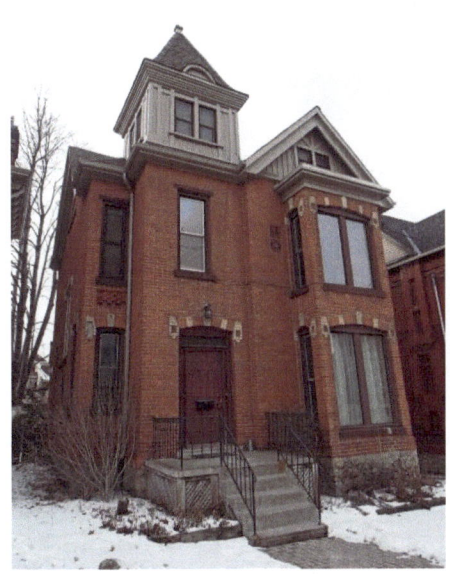

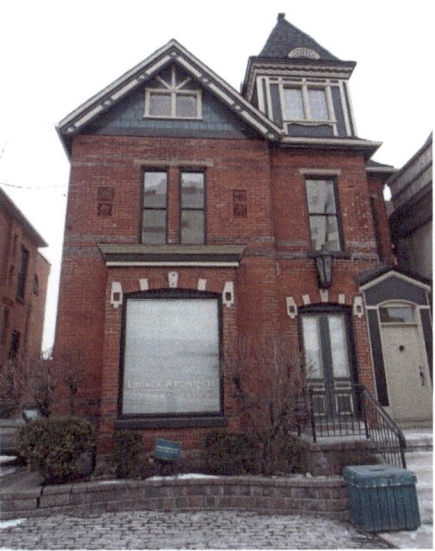

248 James Street South   246 James Street South
Queen Anne style

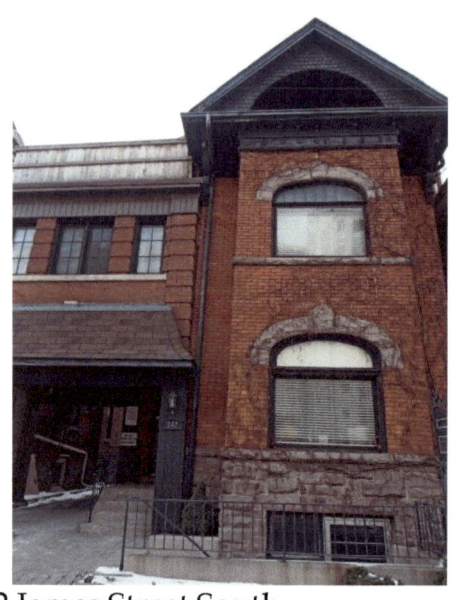
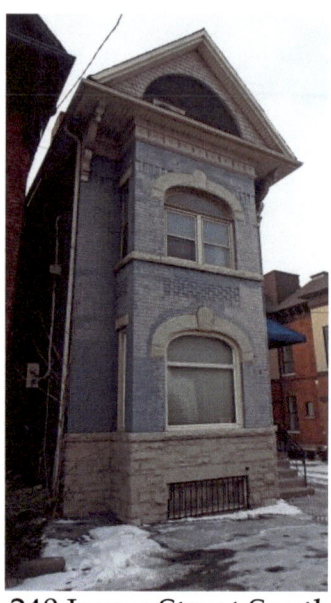

242 James Street South   240 James Street South

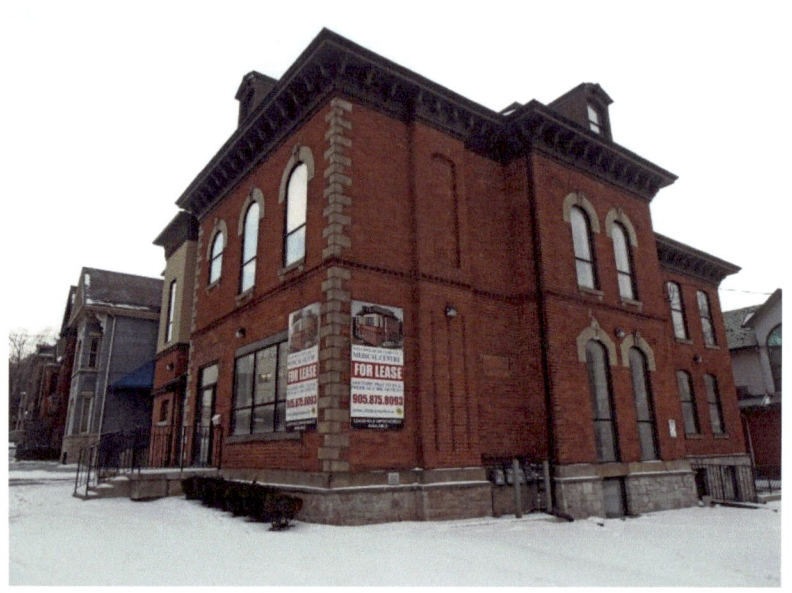

238 James Street South – Italianate, cornice brackets, dormers, corner quoins, window voussoirs and keystones

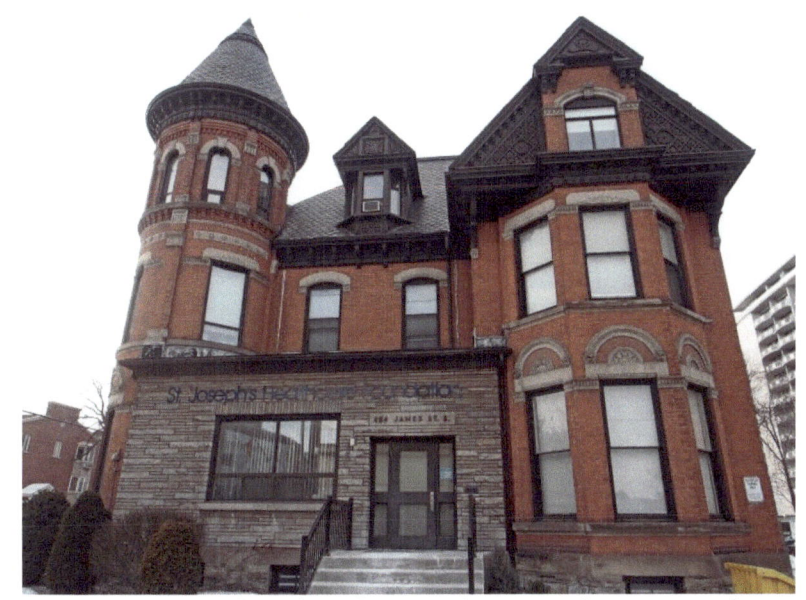

224 James Street South – Queen Anne style, turret, dormer

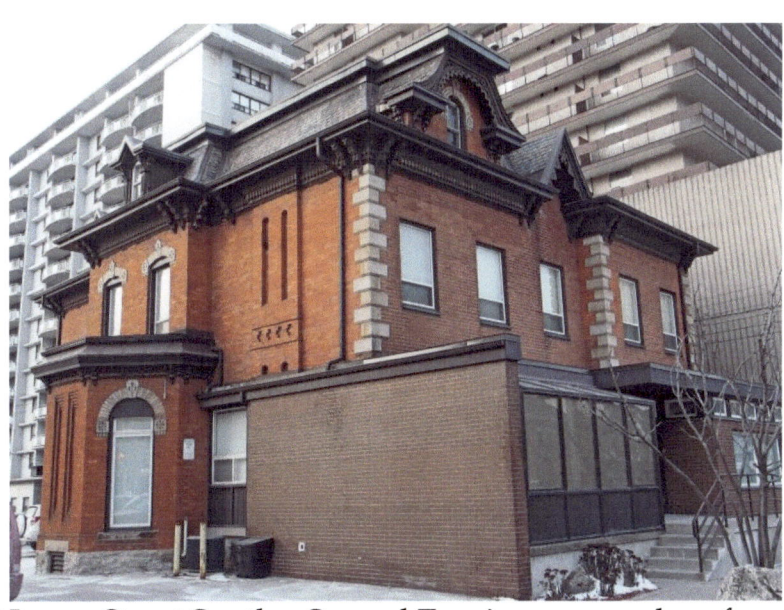

222 James Street South – Second Empire, mansard roof, corner quoins, verge board trim, window voussoirs and keystones

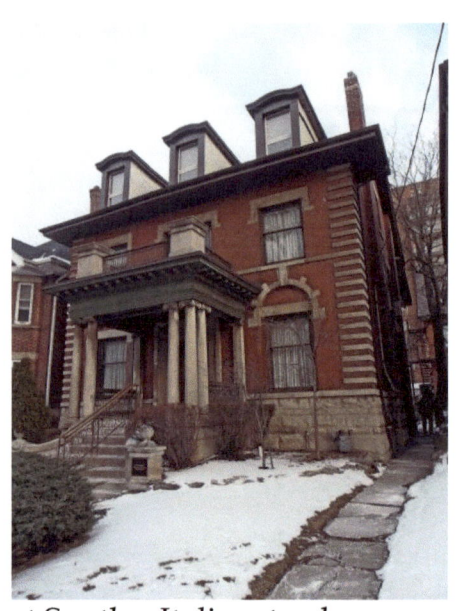

195 James Street South – Italianate, dormers, corner quoins, Ionic capitals on porch pillars, decorative window voussoir

MacNab Street
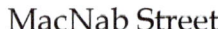

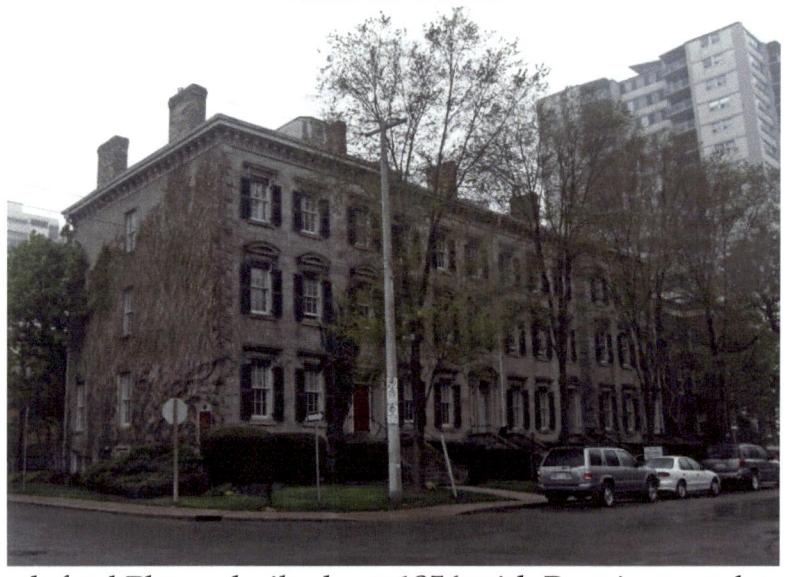

Sandyford Place – built about 1856 with Renaissance details on the windows and door heads; corner quoining

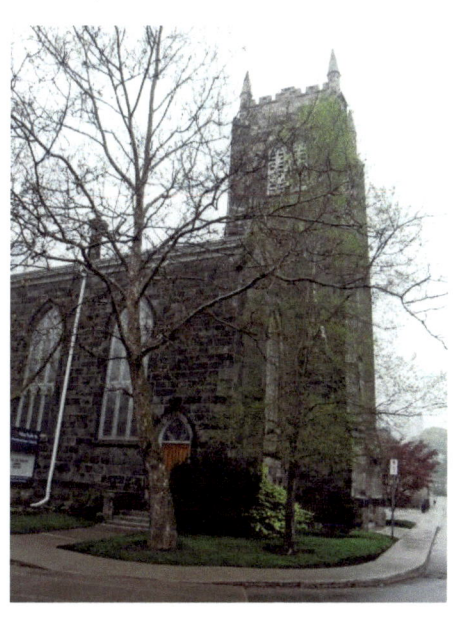

MacNab Street Presbyterian Church

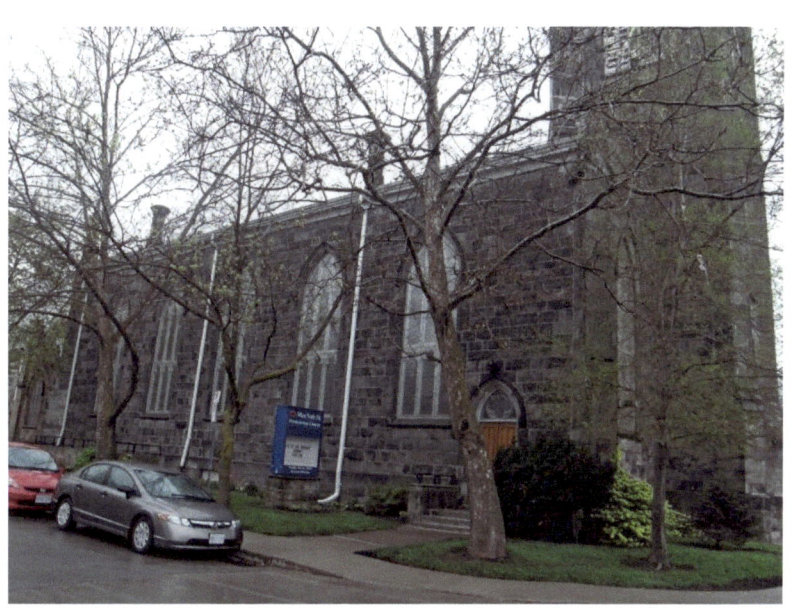

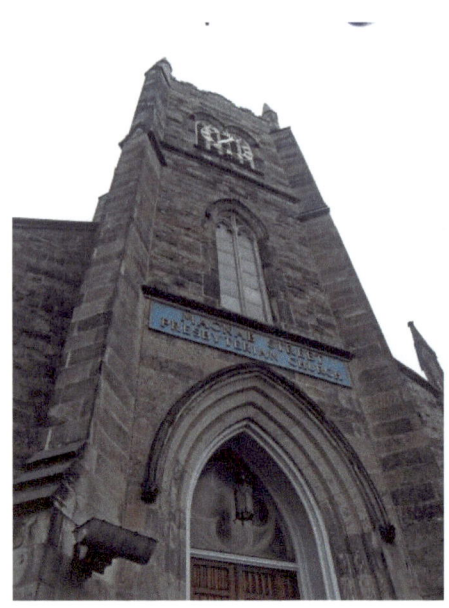
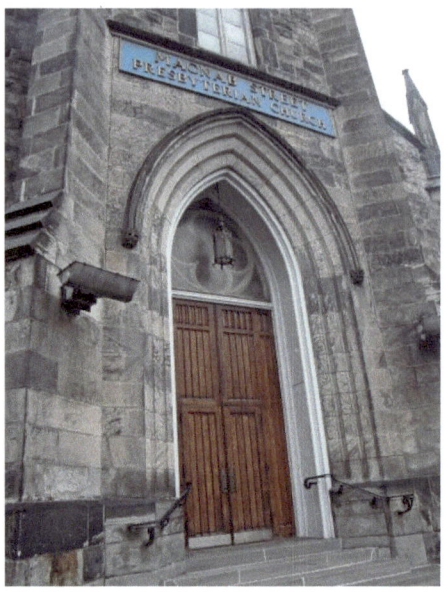

MacNab Street Presbyterian Church

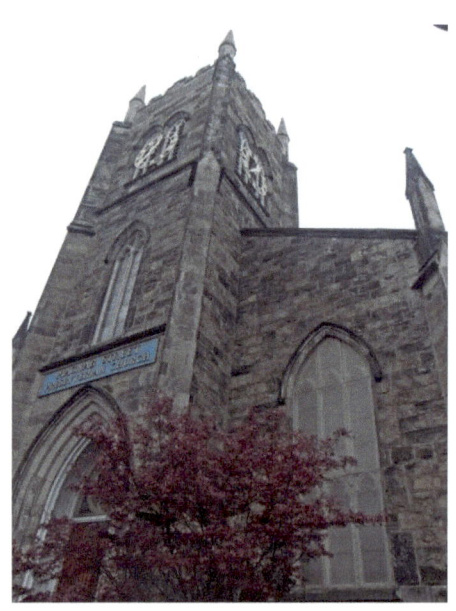

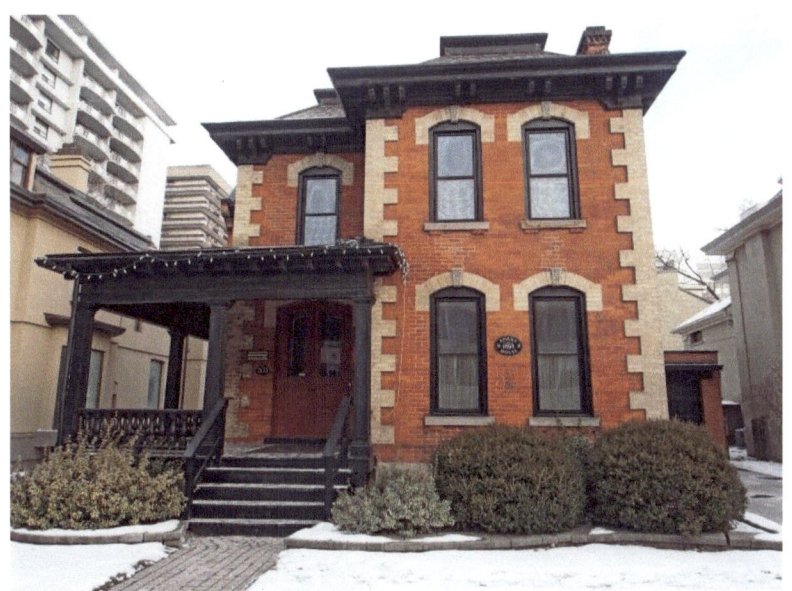

203 MacNab Street South – Italianate, corner quoins
Anaxa House - 1898

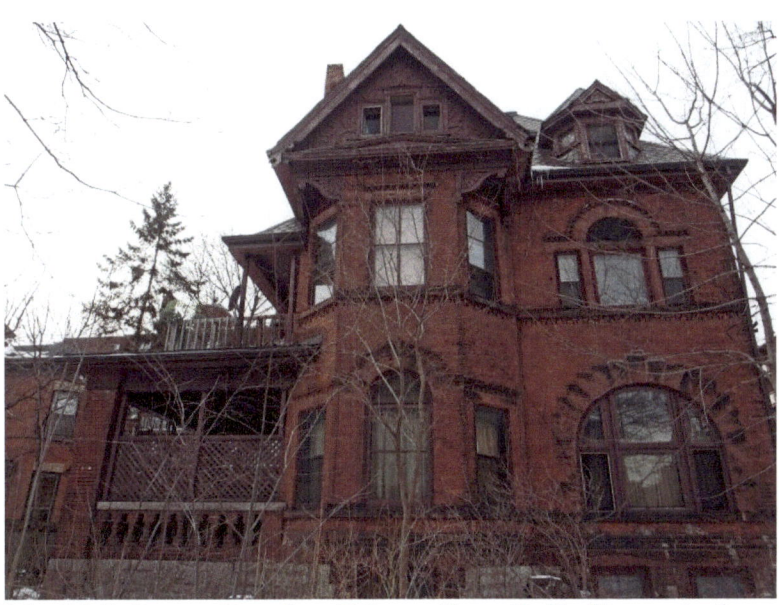

MacNab Street South – Edwardian, Palladian window,
dormer window, Romanesque style window arch

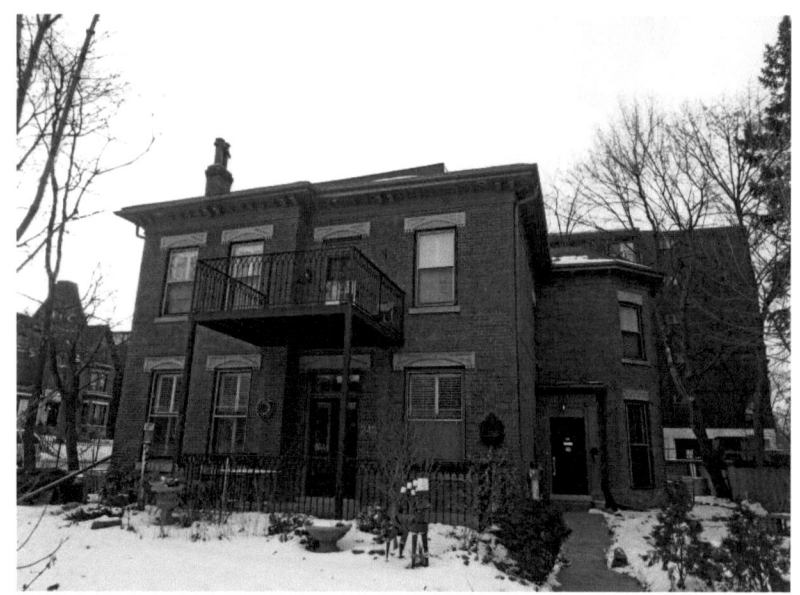

242 MacNab Street South – Italianate, cornice brackets

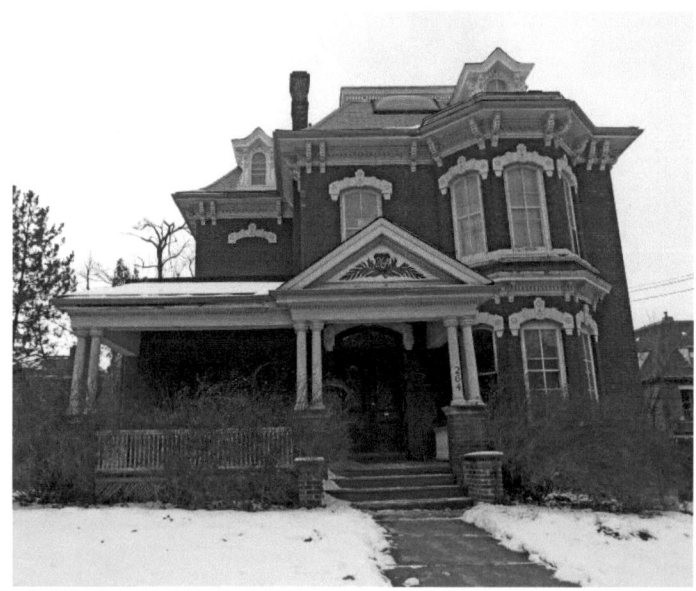

264 MacNab Street South – Second Empire, mansard roof, dormers, cornice brackets, pediment, two-storey bay window

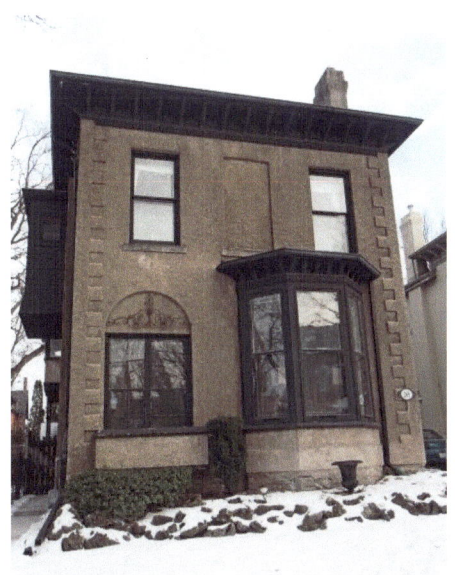

265 MacNab Street South – Italianate, cornice brackets, bay window, corner quoins

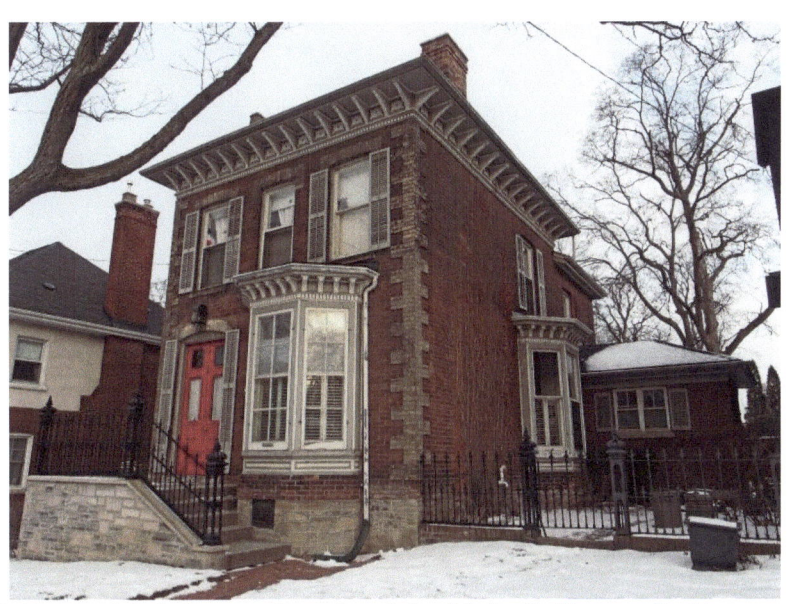

261 MacNab Street South – MacNab Gallery – Italianate, corner quoins, bay windows, cornice brackets

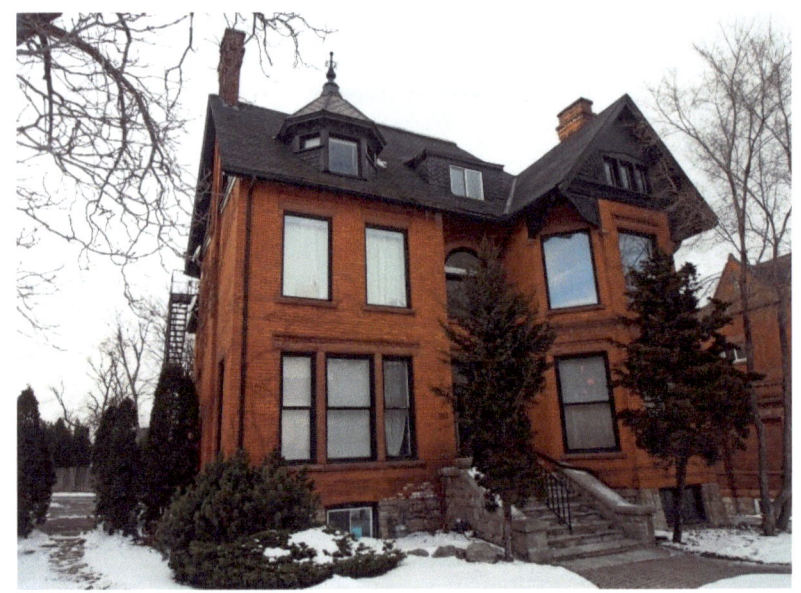

262 MacNab Street South – Edwardian, gretwork

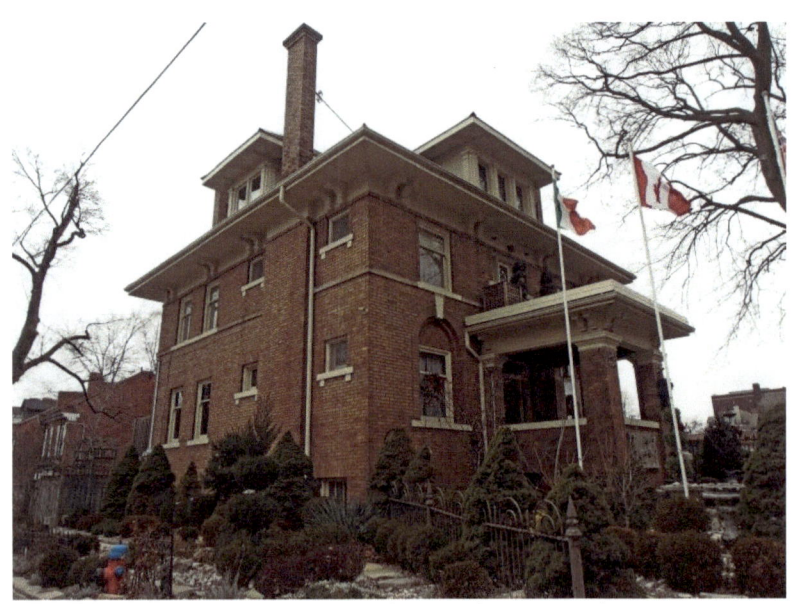

74 Queen Street South – Italianate, dormers

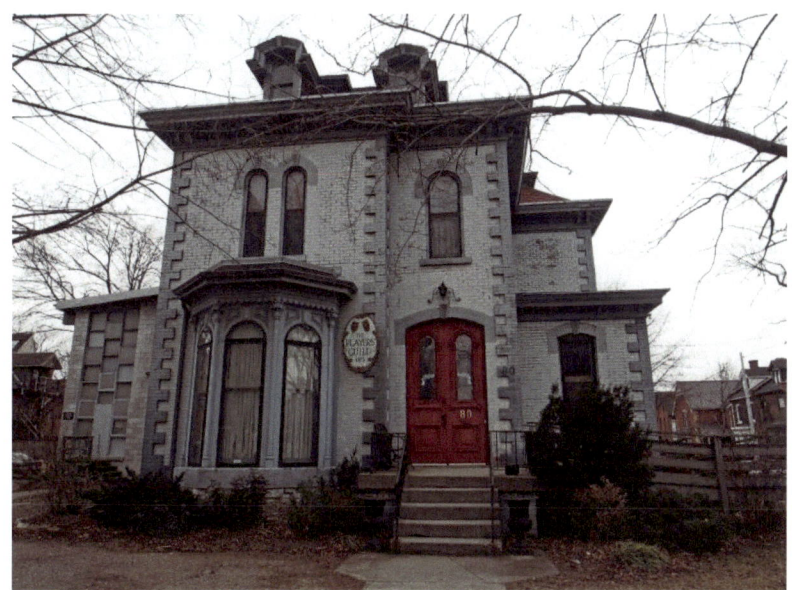

80 Queen Street South – The Players Guild 1875, Italianate, dormers, corner quoining, keystones

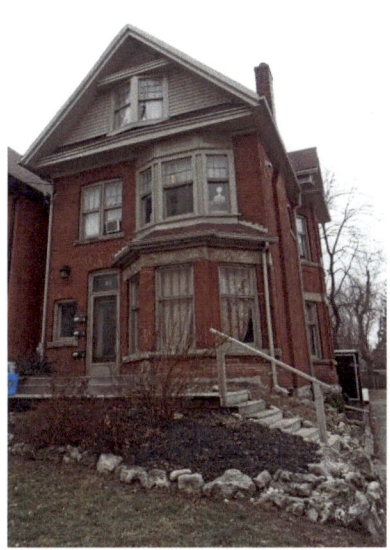

88 Queen Street South   90 Queen Street South
Edwardian, bay windows

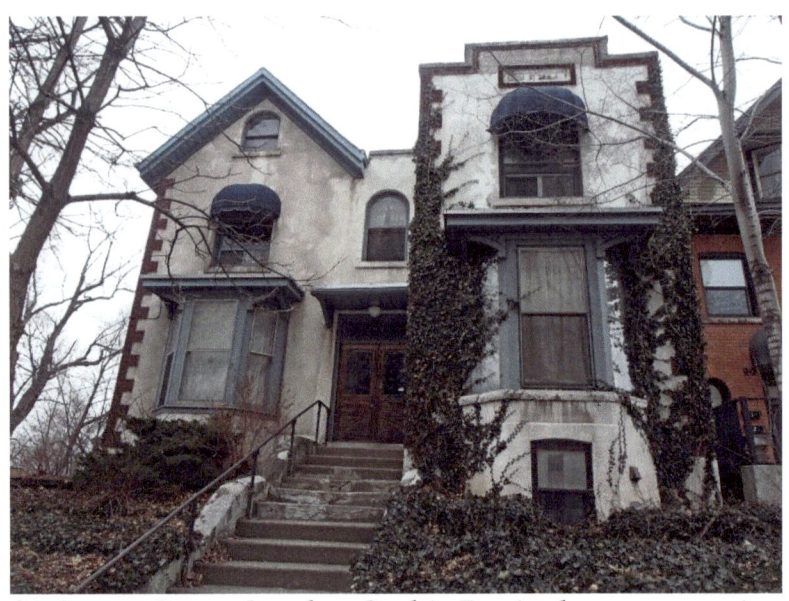

94 Queen Street South – Gothic Revival, corner quoins

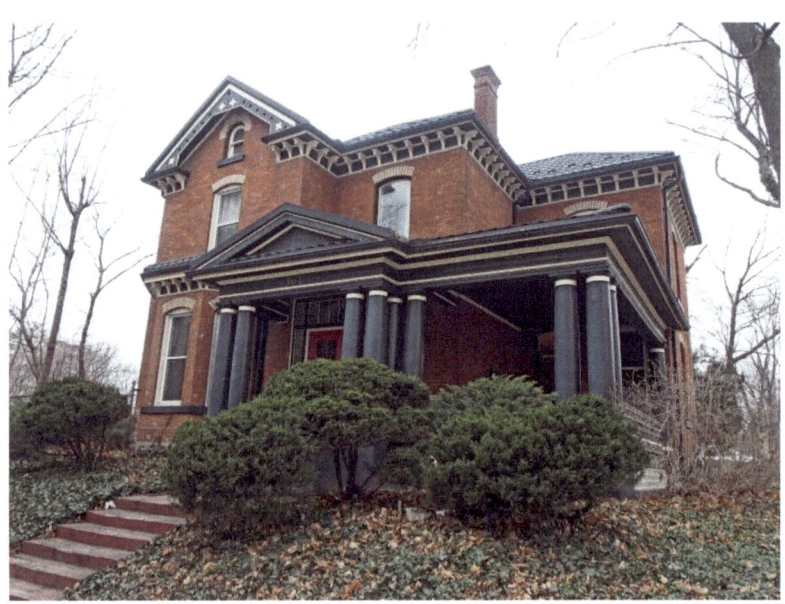

102 Queen Street South – verge board trim, cornice brackets, pediment above wraparound verandah

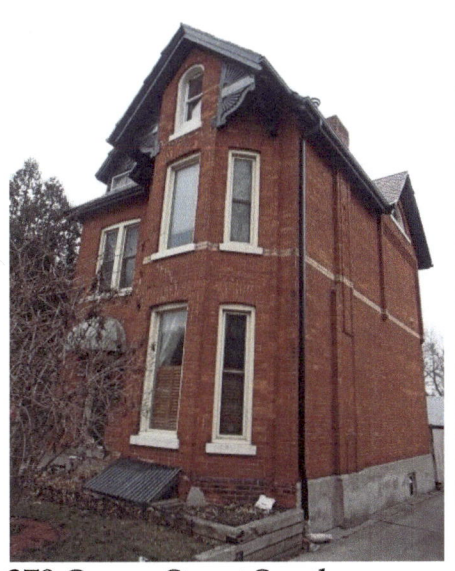

270 Queen Street South
Fretwork

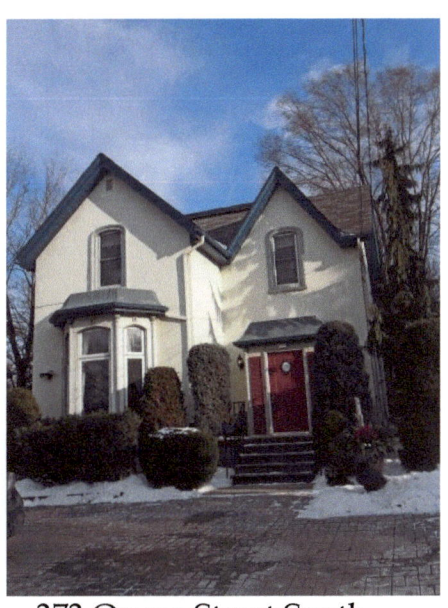

373 Queen Street South
Gothic Revival

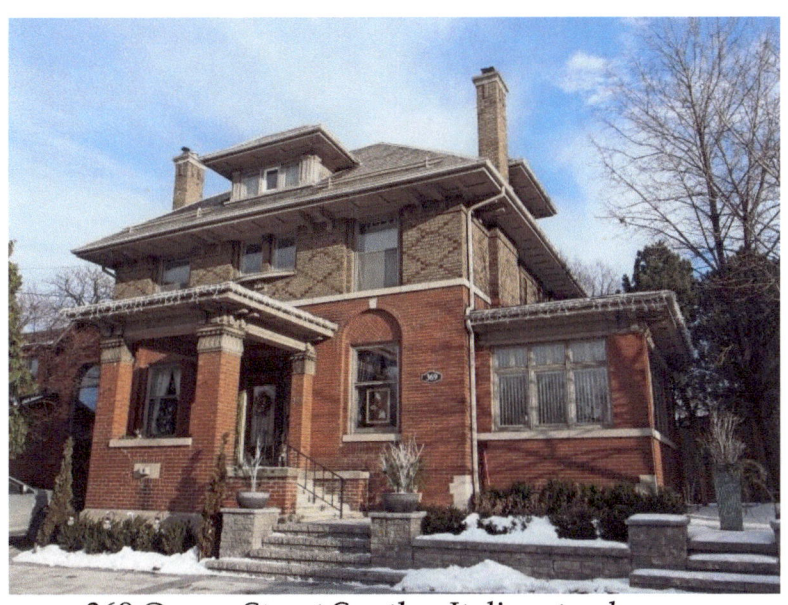

369 Queen Street South – Italianate, dormer

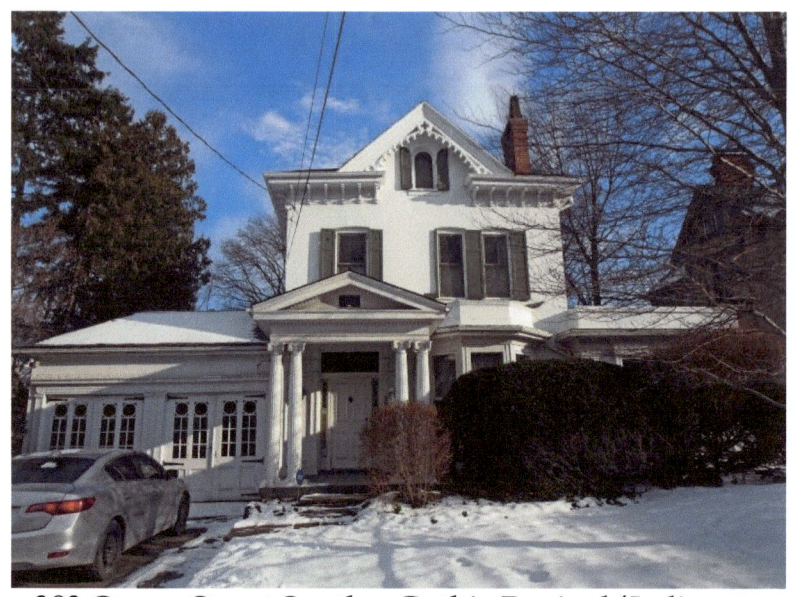

393 Queen Street South – Gothic Revival/Italianate
Verge board trim on gable, pediment, Ionic capitals

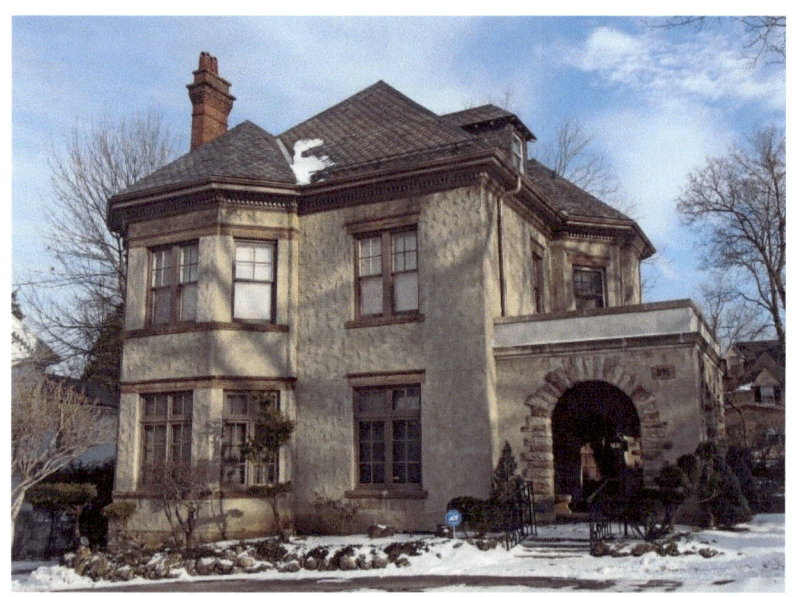

395 Queen Street South - Italianate

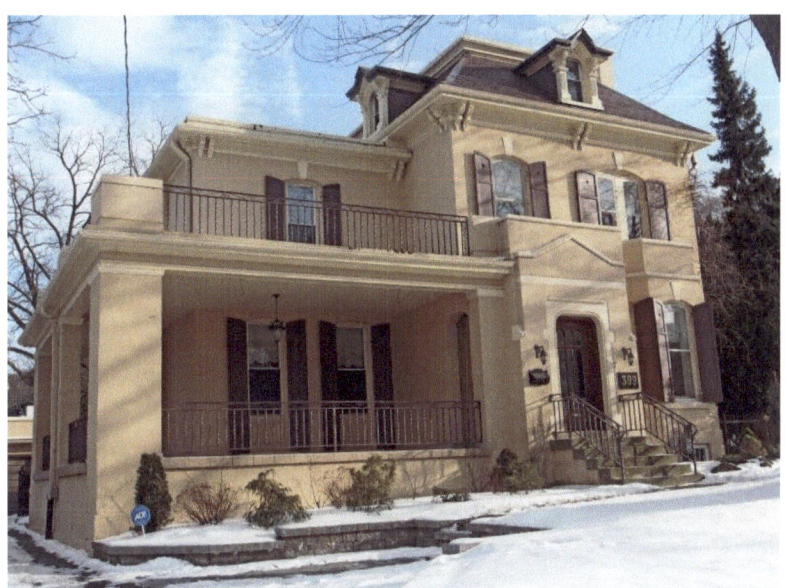

399 Queen Street South – Italianate, dormers, 2nd floor balcony
Paired cornice brackets

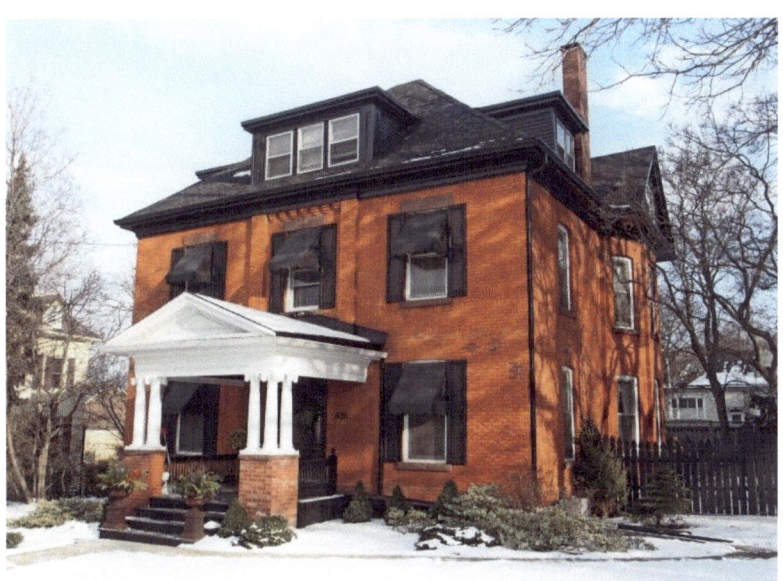

401 Queen Street South – Italianate, dormers, pediment, Ionic
capitals on entrance pillars

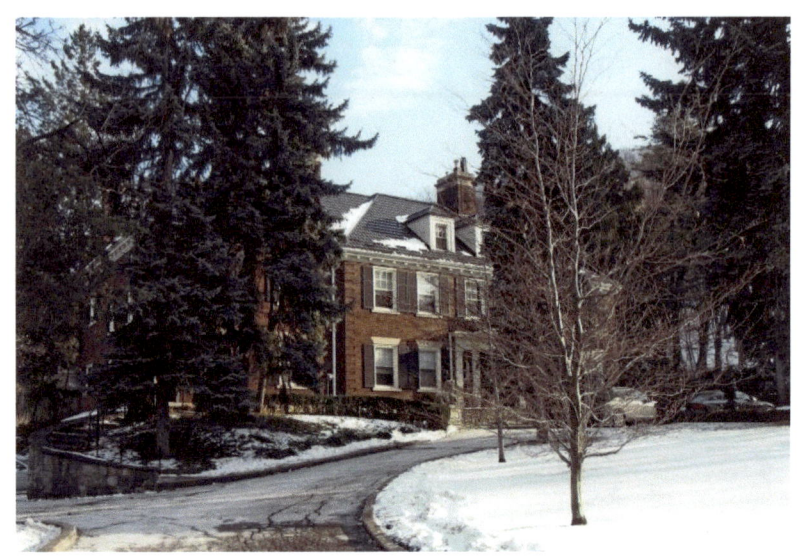

403 Queen Street South

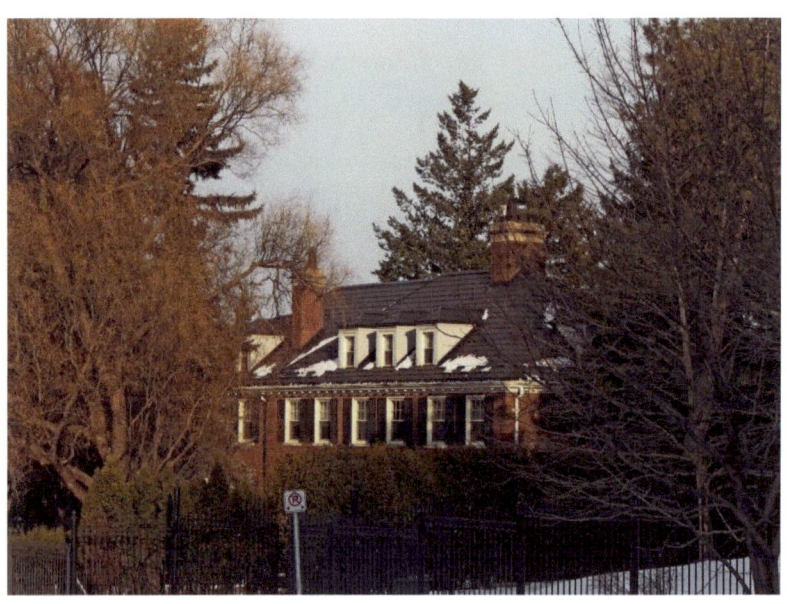

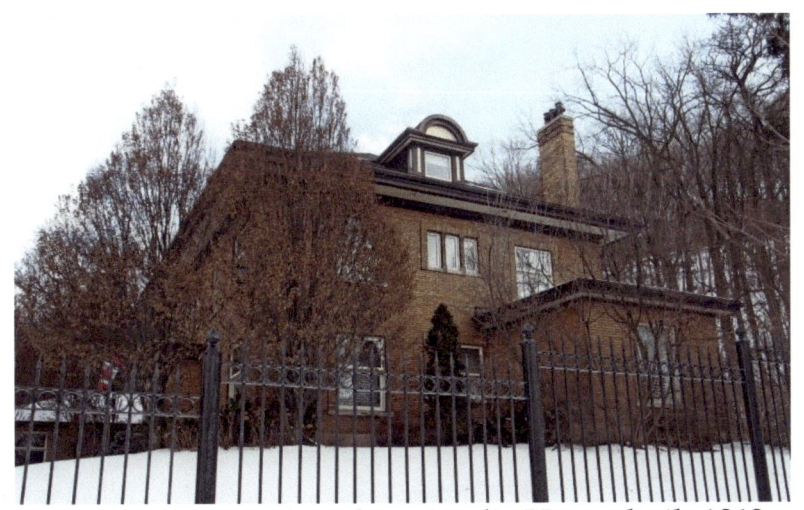

407 Queen Street South – Moodie House built 1913

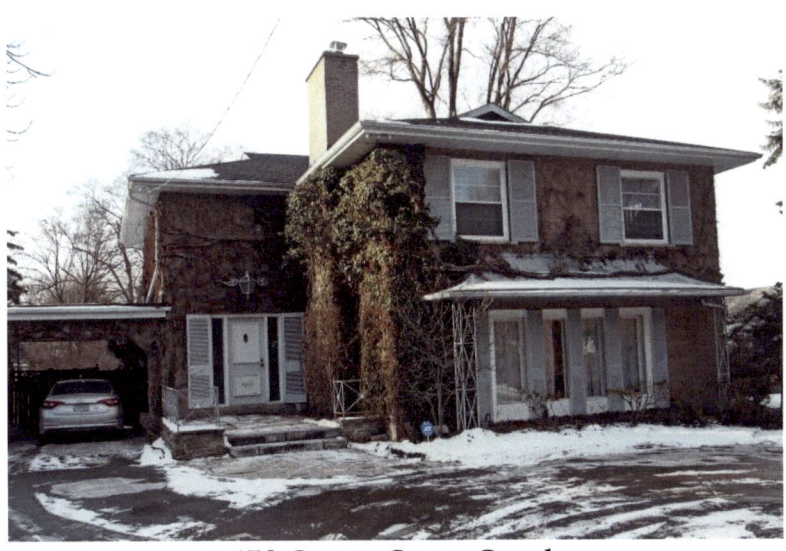

450 Queen Street South

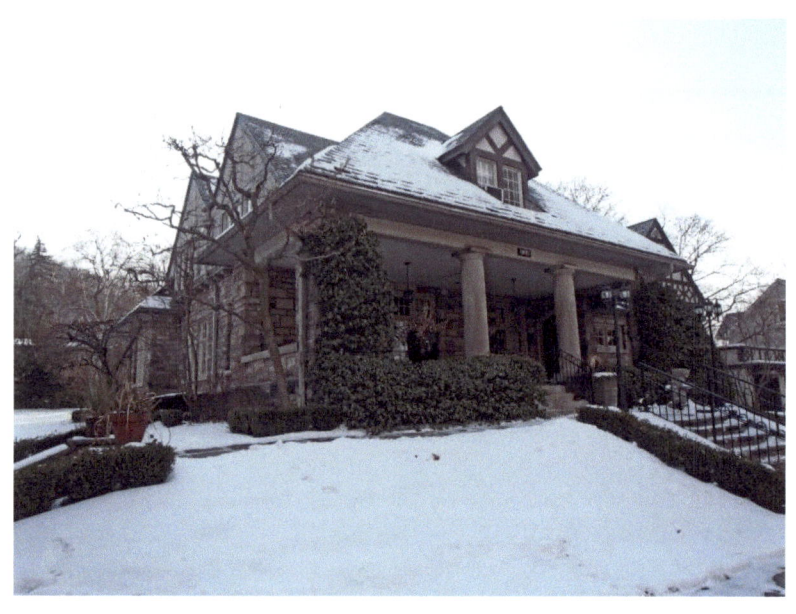

436 Queen Street South – Tudor style

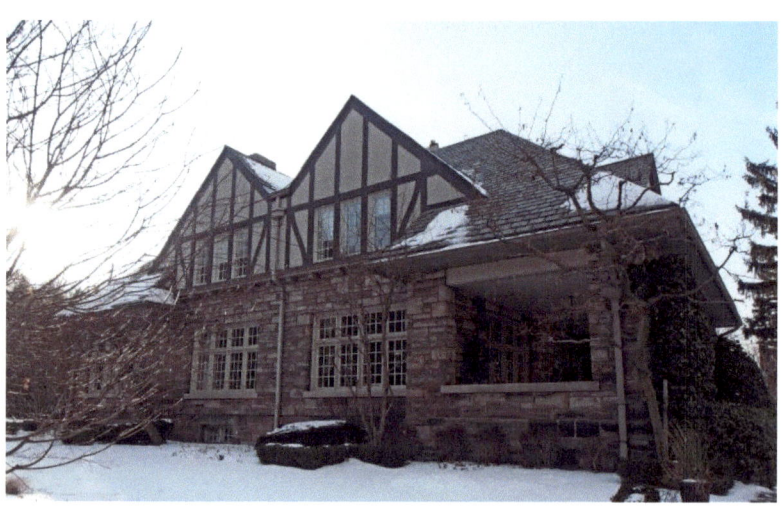

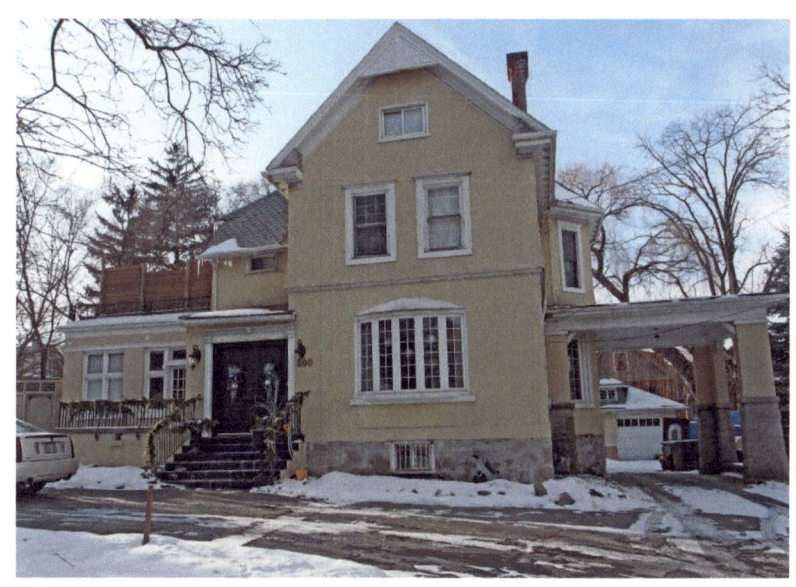

400 Queen Street South – Gothic Revival,
cornice return on gable, dormer

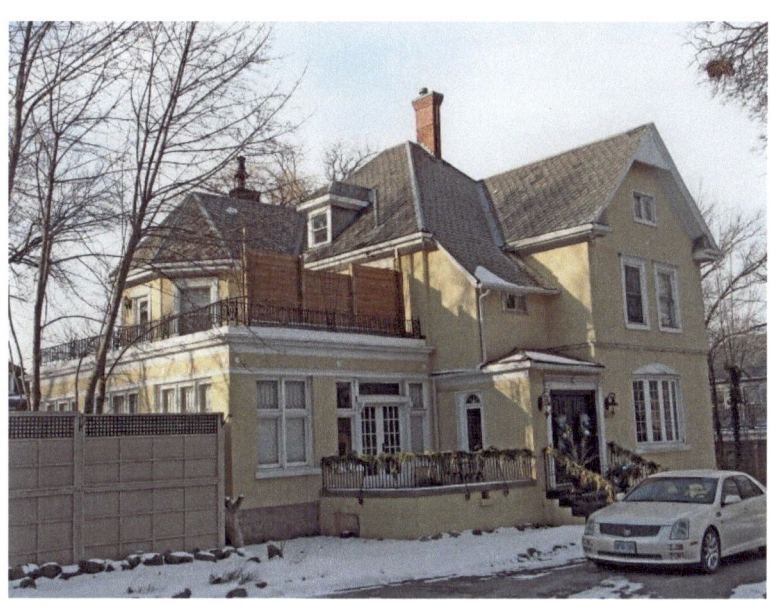

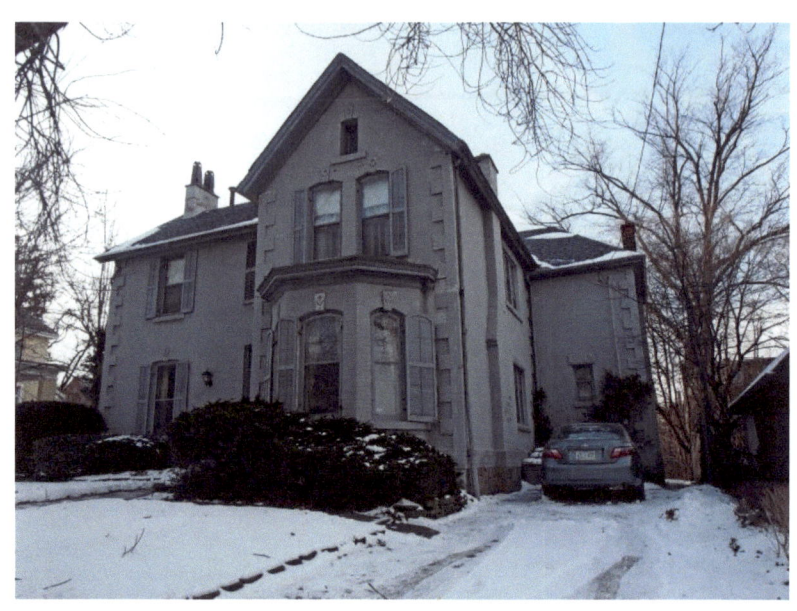

394 Queen Street South - Gothic Revival, corner quoins, bay window

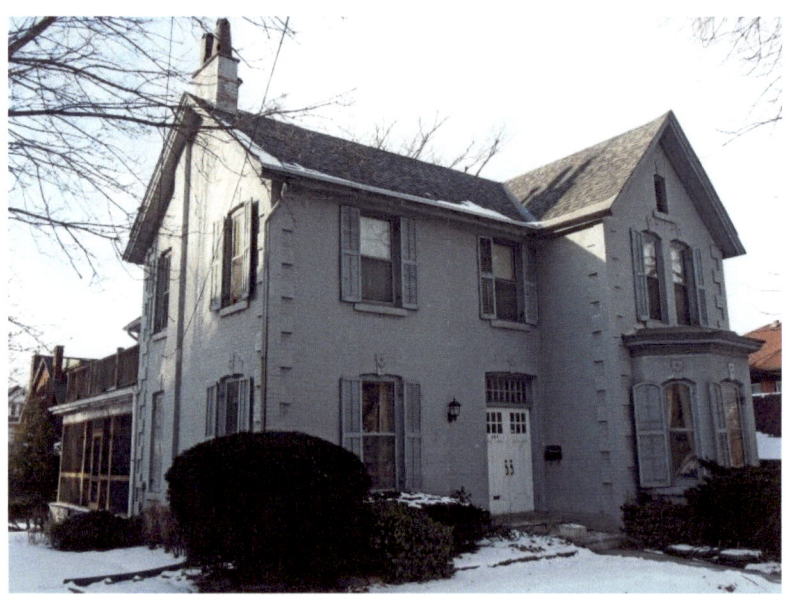

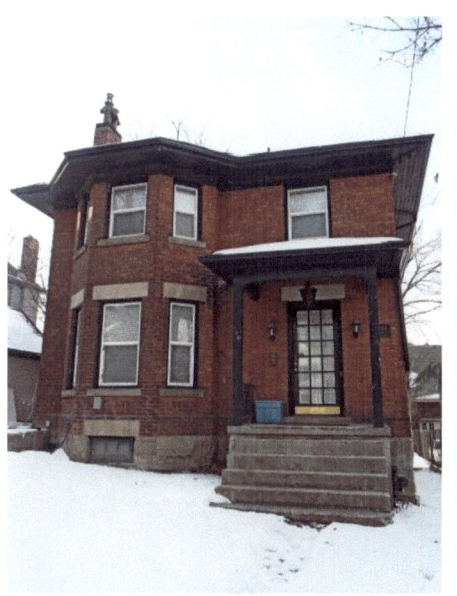

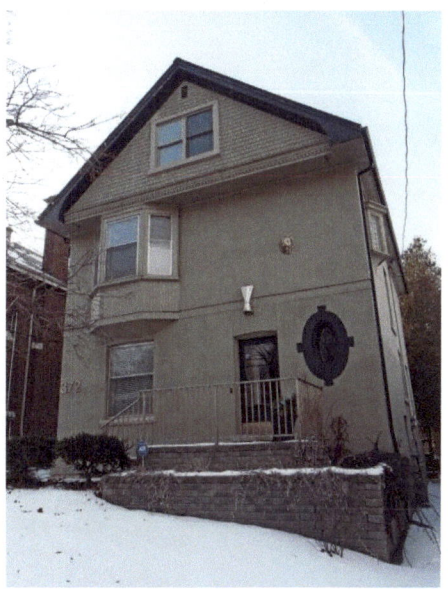

378 Queen Street South
Italianate
Two-storey bay window

372 Queen Street South
Gothic

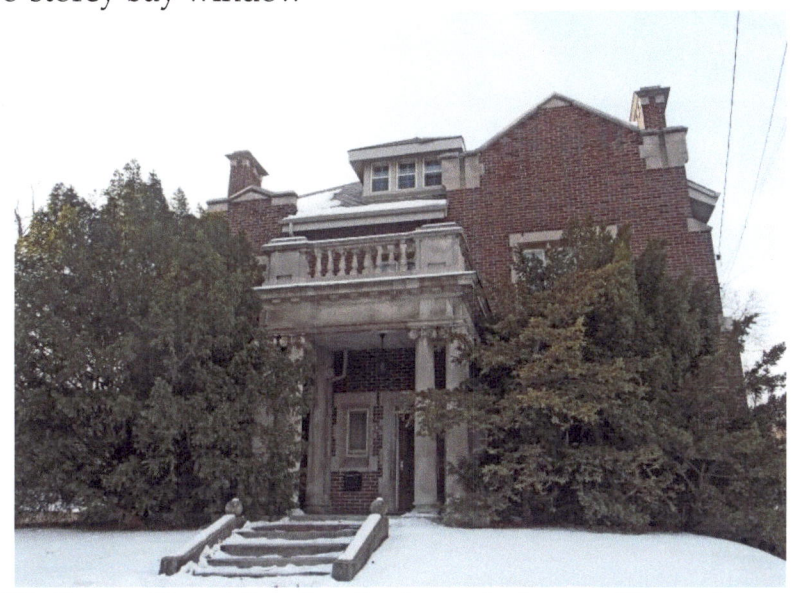

374 Queen Street South – Ionic capitals on pillars, dormer

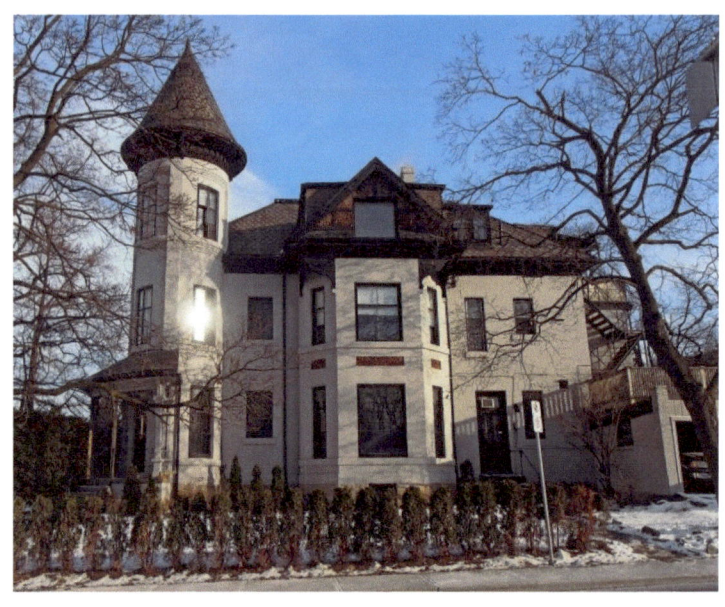

Queen Street South at Aberdeen – Queen Anne style, turret

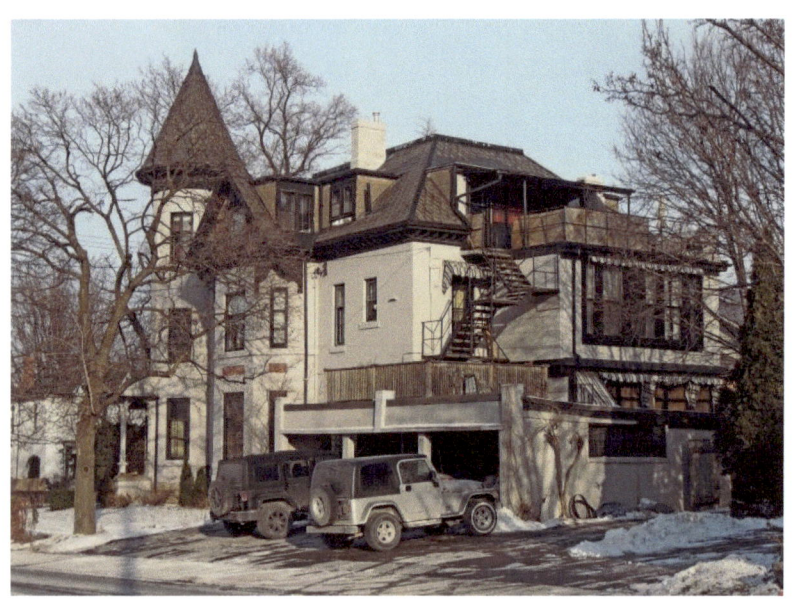

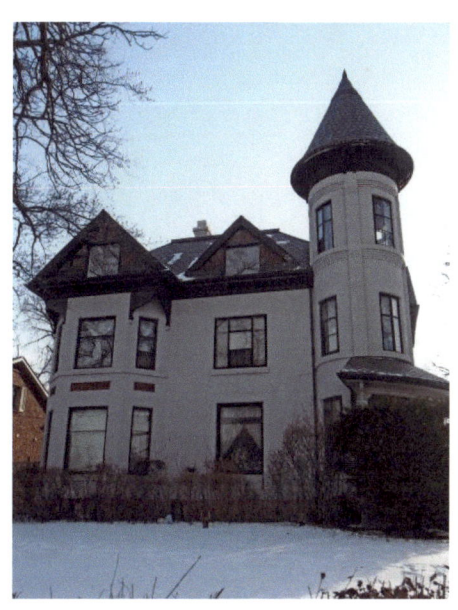

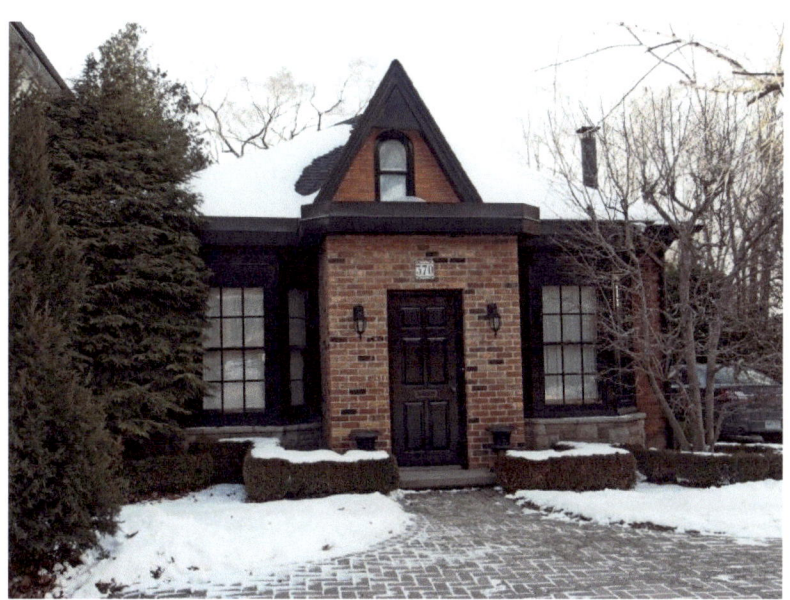

370 Queen Street South - Gothic

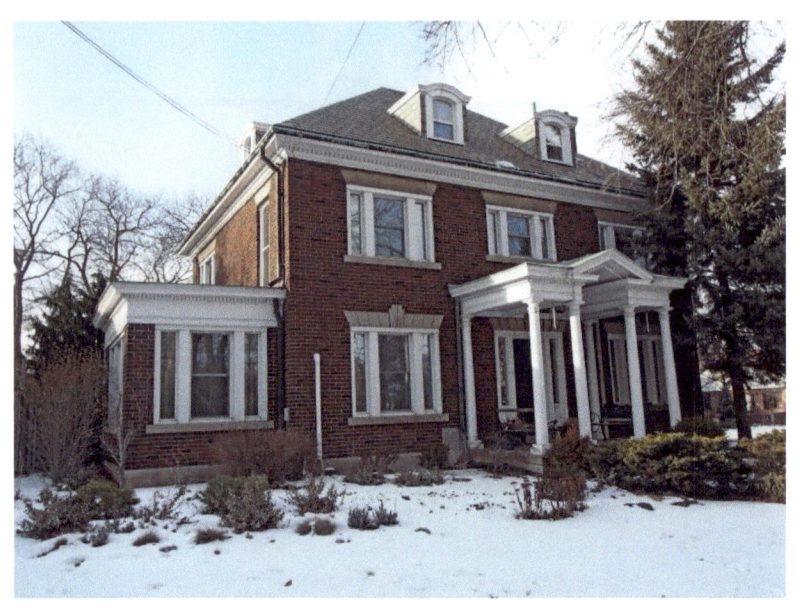

Queen Street South

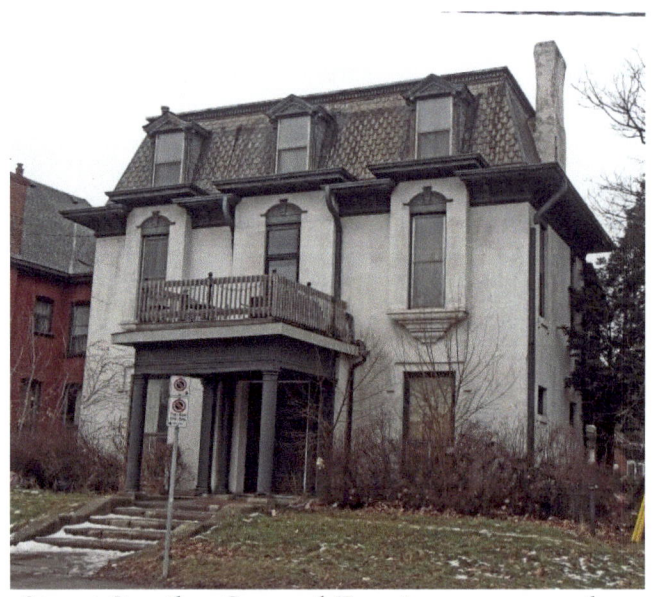

Queen Street South – Second Empire – mansard roof with
dormers, 2nd floor balcony

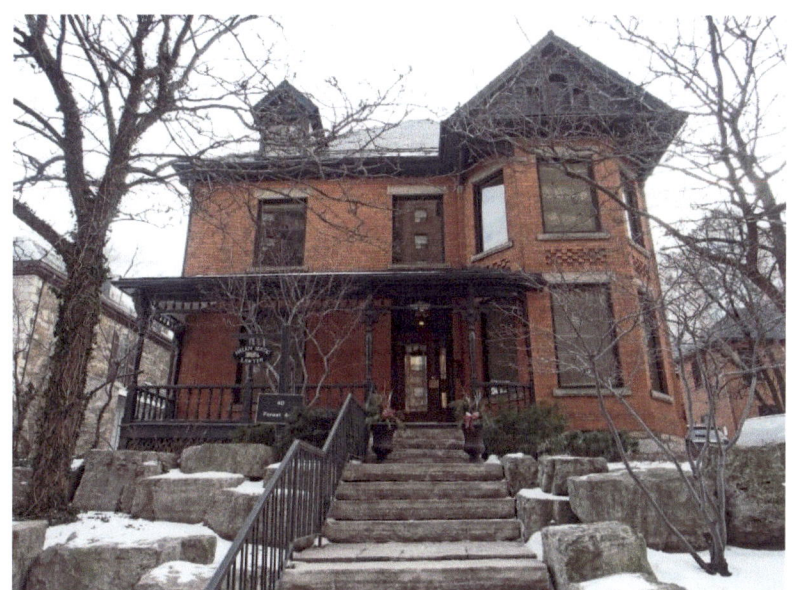

40 Forest Avenue – Edwardian, Palladian window, dormer

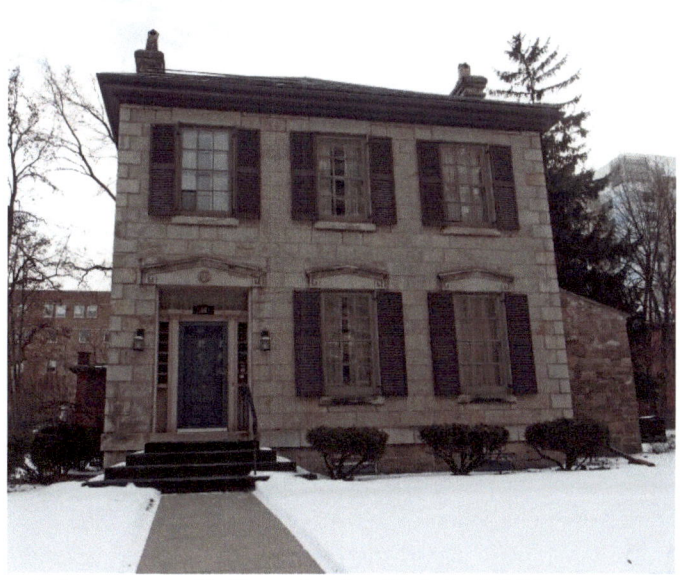

46 Forest Avenue – Italianate, built late 1840s, corner quoins

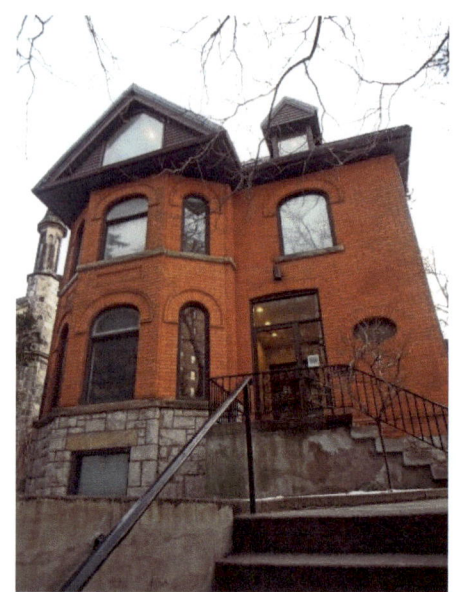

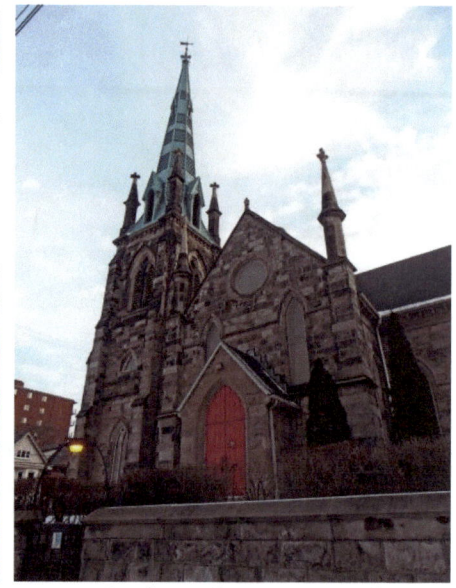

50 Forest Avenue   rose window, lancet windows

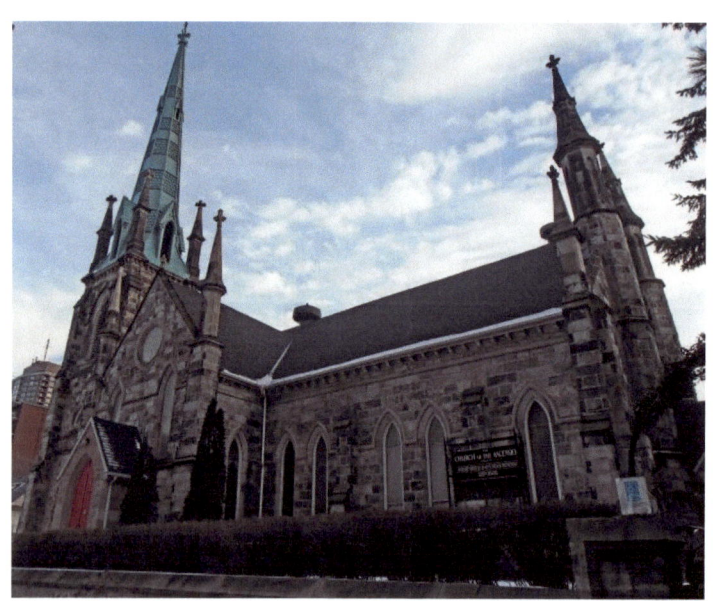

Forest Avenue – Anglican Church of the Ascension

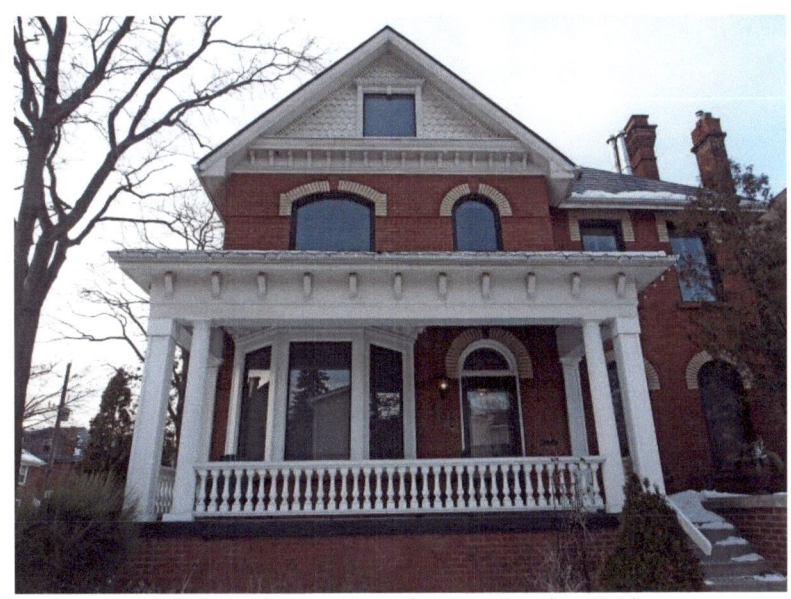

290 Hess Street South – arched window
voussoirs with keystones

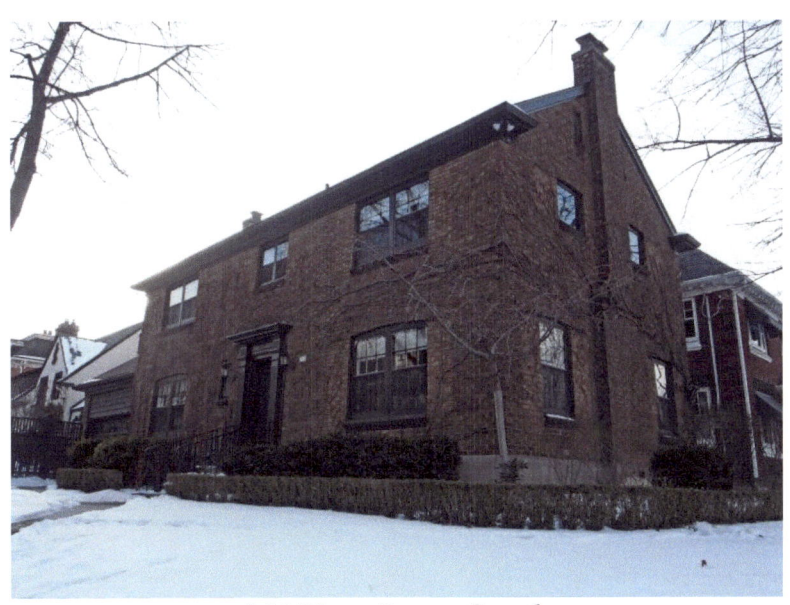

364 Hess Street South

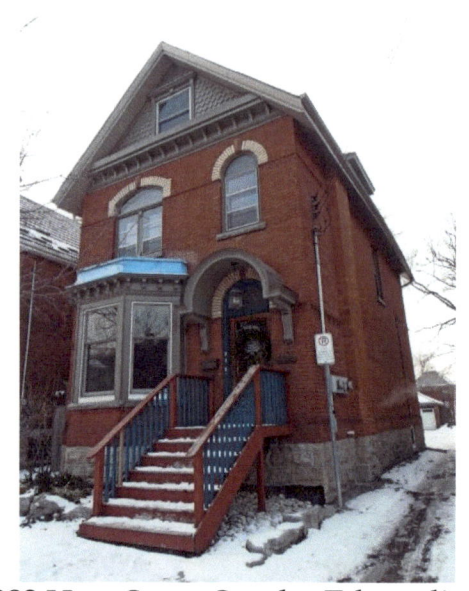

282 Hess Street South - Edwardian

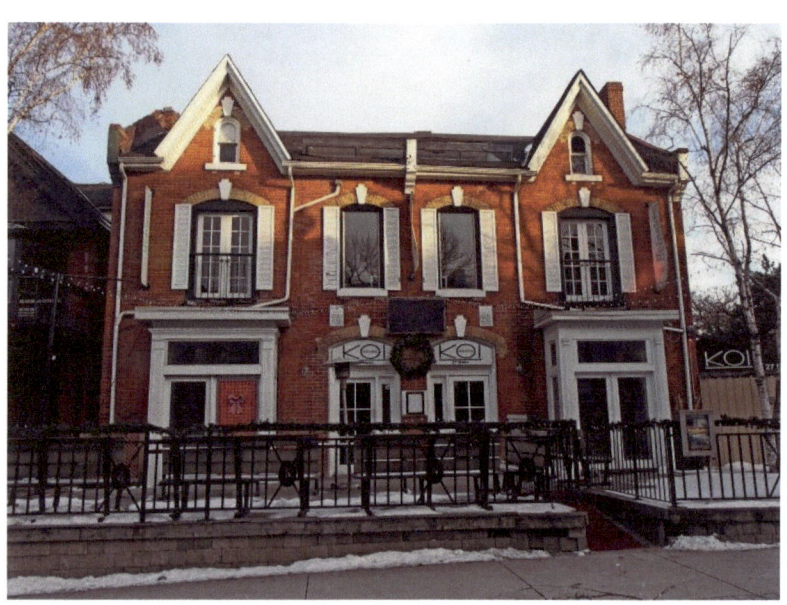

27 Hess Street South – Gothic Revival, keystones

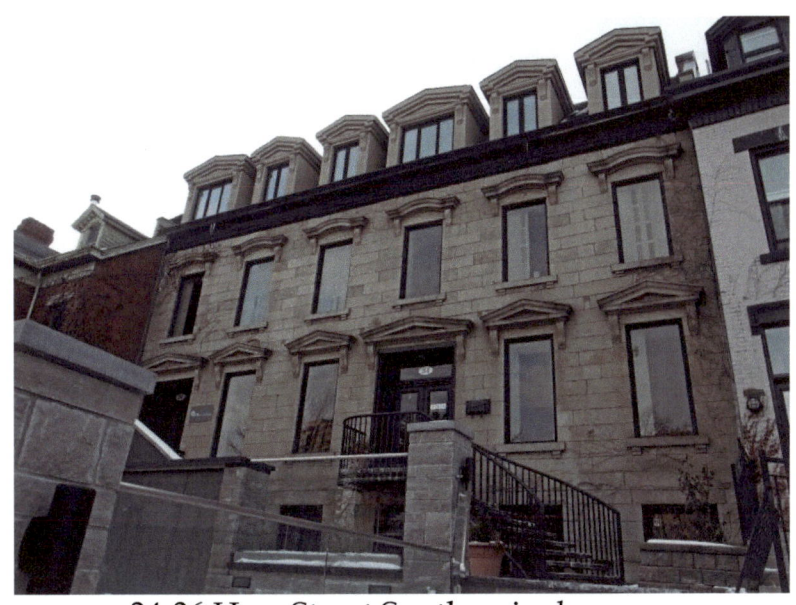

34-36 Hess Street South – six dormers,

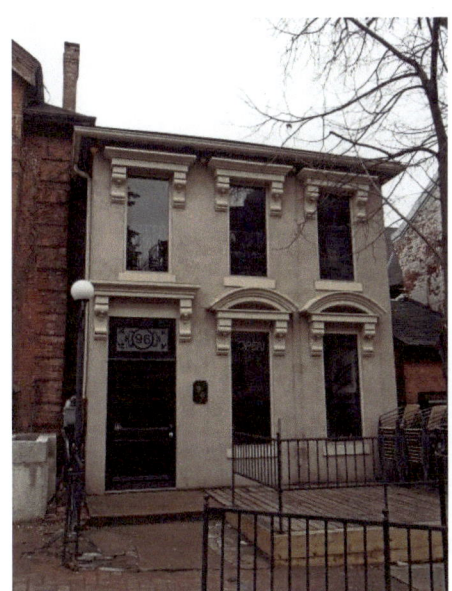

96 Hess Street South
Italianate

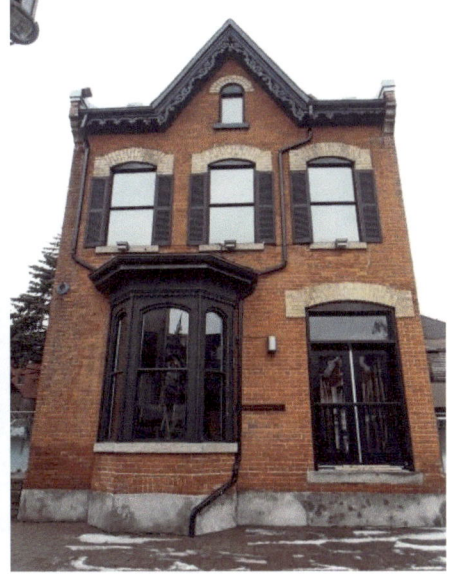

Hess Street South
Gothic Revival, verge board

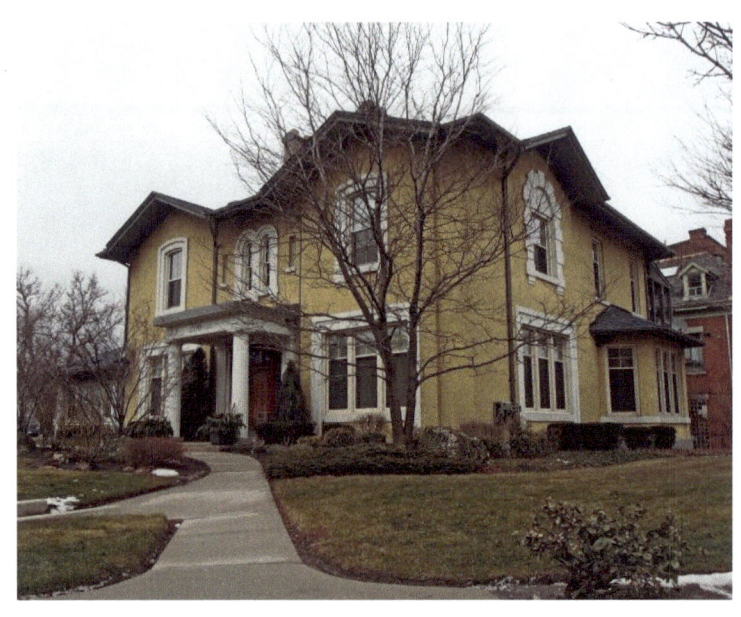

206 Main Street West at Hess – Arlo House – Gothic Revival

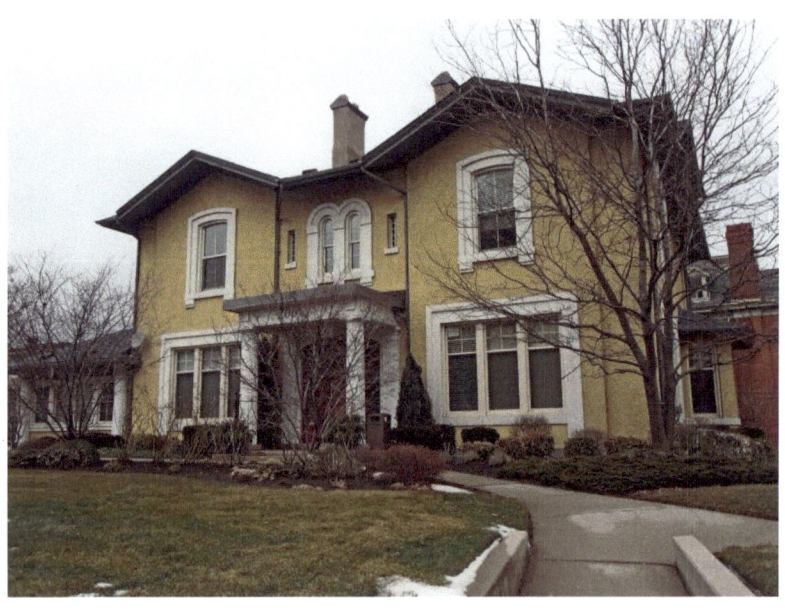

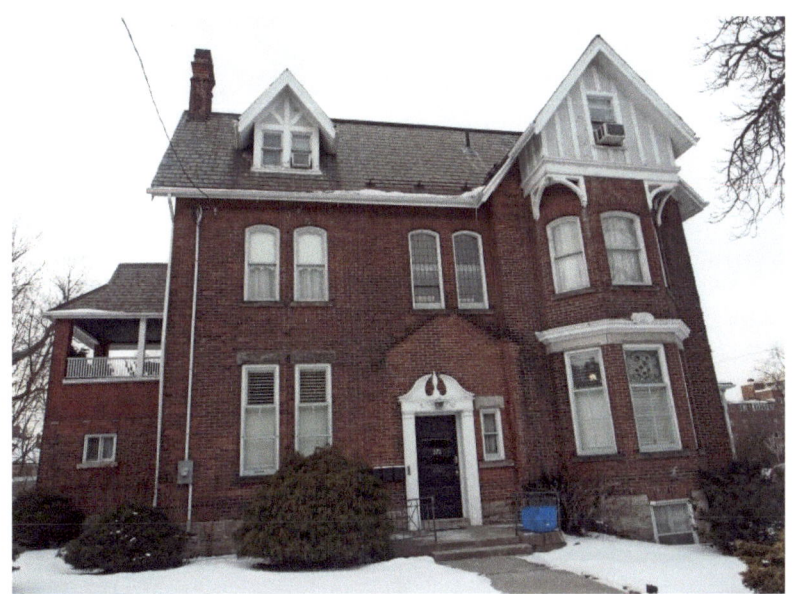

272 Park Street South – Ivy Manor – fretwork, 2½ storey
tower-like bay, dormer

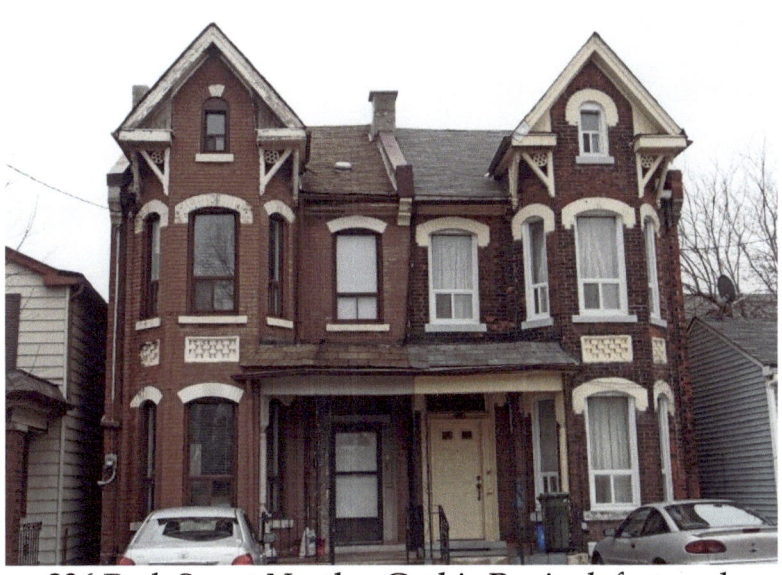

236 Park Street North – Gothic Revival, fretwork

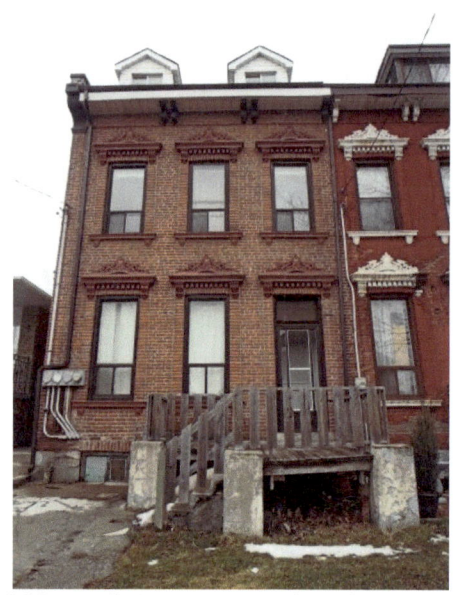

223 Park Street North - dormers

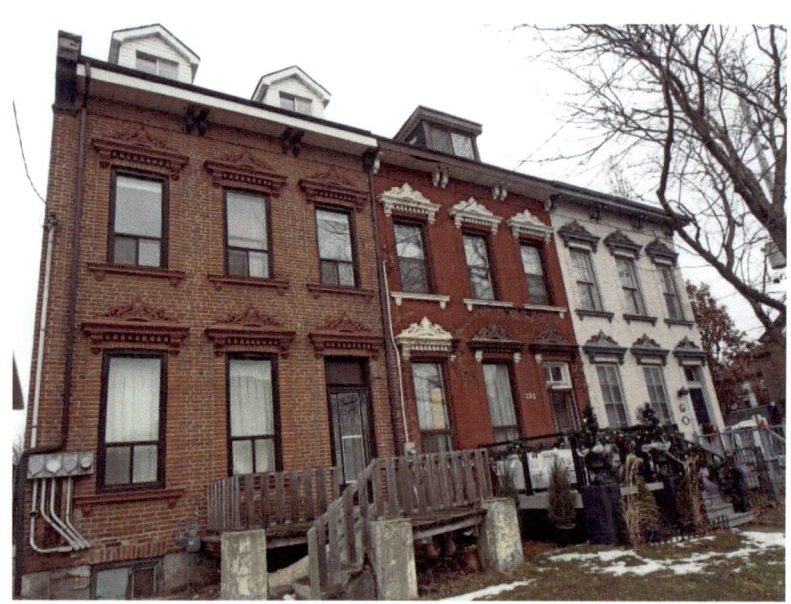

223-227 Park Street North – decorative window hoods

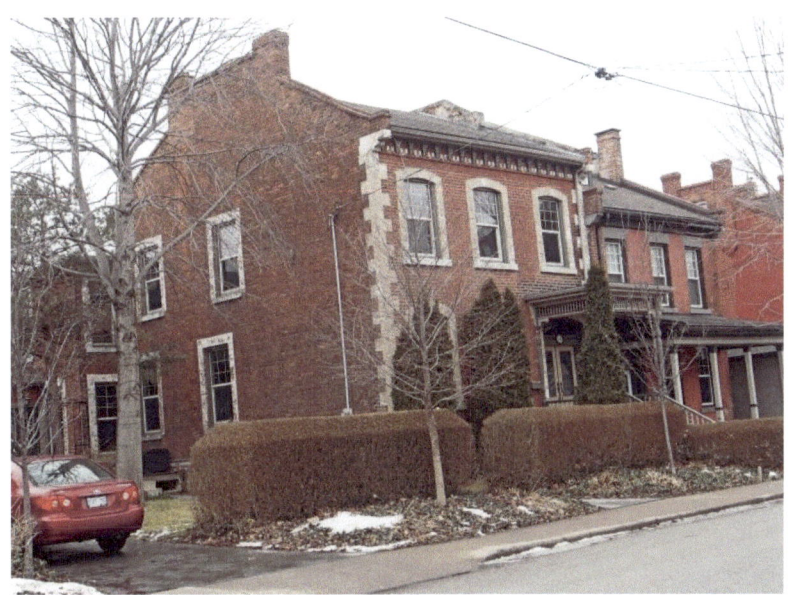

239 Park Street North – corner quoins, cornice brackets

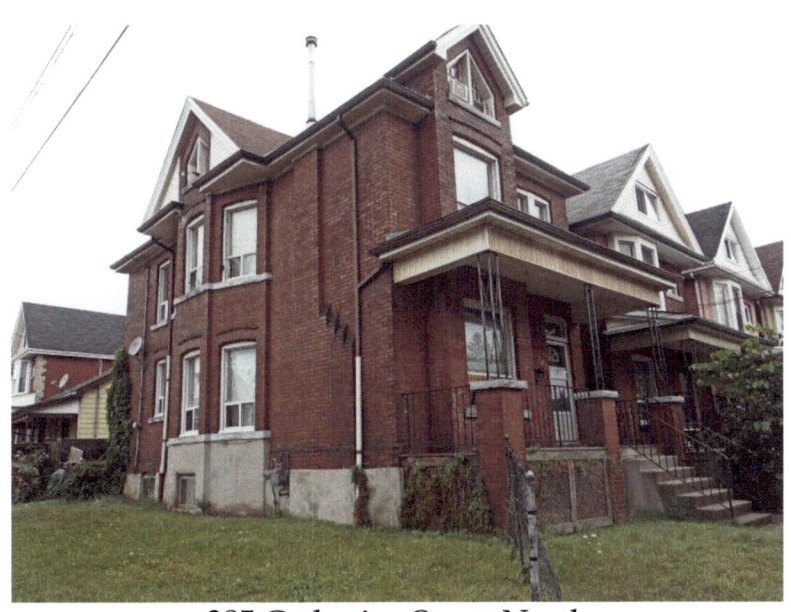

385 Catharine Street North

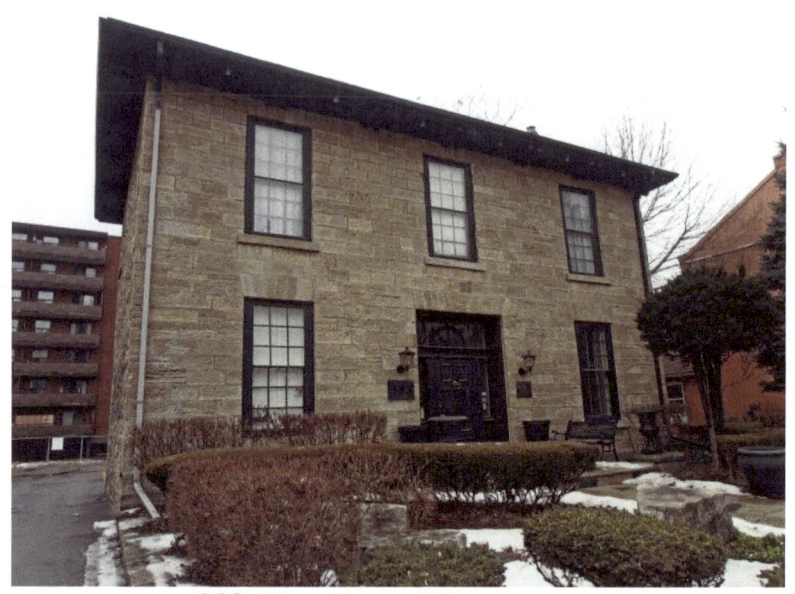

393 King Street West - stone

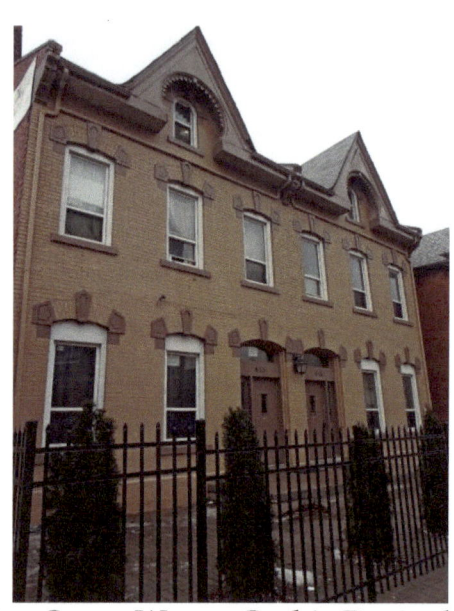

413-415 King Street West – Gothic Revival, keystones

Architectural Terms

Bay Window: A window that projects out from a wall, in a semicircular, rectangular, or polygonal design. Used frequently in Gothic and Victorian designs. Example: 46 Herkimer Street	
Brackets: a decorative or weight-bearing structural element which forms a right angle with one side against a wall and the other under a projecting surface such as an eave or roof. Example: 178 Herkimer Street	
Buttress: a masonry structure built against or projecting from a wall which serves to support or reinforce the wall. In Canadian architecture, they are sometimes used for decoration. Example: Basilica of Christ the King	
Capital: The uppermost finish or decoration on a column. An Ionic column has a small base, a thin elegant shaft, and a capital composed of volutes which are carved whirls or twists that take the form of a scroll. Example: 221 Herkimer Street	
Dormer: (French for "sleep") a gable end window that pierces through the plane of a sloping roof surface to create usable space in the top floor or attic of a building by adding headroom. Example: 146 Herkimer Street	
Entrance: The entrance encompasses the doorway and the inner vestibule or, in residential architecture, the covered porch. Example: 46 Herkimer	

Gable: the triangular portion of a wall between the edges of a sloping roof. Example: 178 Herkimer Street	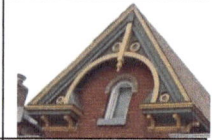
Keystones and Voussoirs: a voussoir is a wedge-shaped element used in building an arch. A keystone is the central stone that locks all the stones into position, allowing the arch to bear weight. Example: 229-231 Kent Street	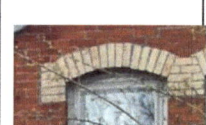
Lancet Window: a tall, narrow window with a pointed arch at its top. Example: 260 Herkimer Street	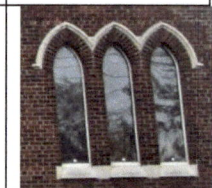
Mansard Roof: This style was popularized by Francois Mansart (1598-1666), an accomplished architect of the French Baroque period and especially fashionable during the Second French Empire (1852-1870). This roof is almost flat on the top section, with two slopes on each of its sides with the lower slope at a steeper angle than the upper and having dormer windows. Example: Queen Street South (see Page 44)	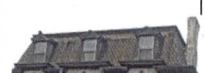
Palladian Window: a large window that is divided into three sections with the centre section larger than the two side sections and usually arched. Example: MacNab Street South (see Page 27)	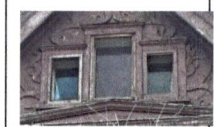
Pediment: a triangular section above the horizontal structure (entablature), typically supported by columns. The inside of the triangle is called the tympanum. Example: 264 MacNab Street South	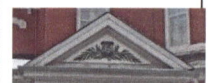

Quoin: masonry blocks at the corner of a wall, often a decorative feature, usually larger or of a different colour than the rest of the wall. Example: 222 James Street South	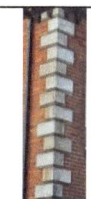
Rose Window: a circular window with ornamental tracery radiating from the centre. Example: 260 Herkimer Street, St. Joseph's Roman Catholic Church	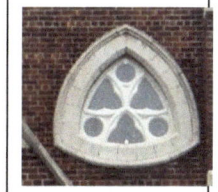
Turret: a small tower that projects from the wall of a building. Example: 224 James Street South	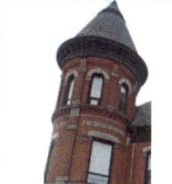
Verge board and Finial: also called bargeboards – hang from the projecting end of a roof and are often elaborately carved and ornamented. **Finial:** ornament added to the top of a gable, pinnacle, canopy or spire – a Gothic element. Example: 229 Kent Street	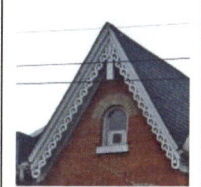
Window Hood: A **hood** is the piece found above window openings, usually of an ornate design, and covers the top third of the opening. Hoods are commonly placed above arched or curved openings on both windows and doors. Example: 316 James Street South	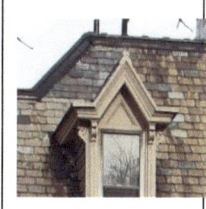

Building Styles

Edwardian, 1900-1930 – This style bridges the ornate and elaborate styles of the Victorian era and the simplified styles of the 20th century. Balanced facades, simple roof lines, dormer windows, large front porches, and smooth brick surfaces are its characteristics. Example: 156 Herkimer Street	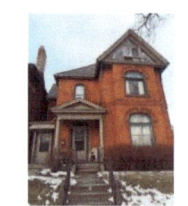
Gothic Revival, 1830-1890 – These decorative buildings have sharply-pitched gables with highly detailed verge boards, pointed-arch window openings, and dichromatic brickwork. It is a common style in Ontario. Example: 229-231 Kent Street	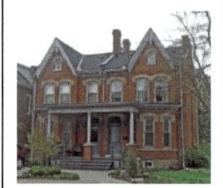
Italianate, 1850-1900 – It has wide-bracketed eaves, belvederes, wrap-around verandahs. Example: 74 Queen Street South	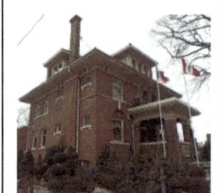
Neo-Classical (1810 - 1850) – This style was a direct result of the War of 1812. Many Upper Canadians returning from the war with the United States were second or third generation Loyalists who had inherited land and means from their forefathers. Once the conflict had passed, they had the money and the time to expand their holdings and indulge their architectural whims. Both residential and commercial buildings were constructed on the traditional Georgian plan, but they had a new gaiety and light-heartedness. Detailing became more refined, delicate, and elegant. Example: 124 Herkimer Street	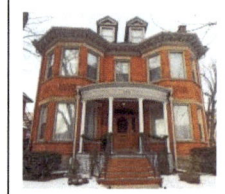

Queen Anne, 1885-1900 – This style is distinguished by an irregular outline featuring a combination of an offset tower, broad gables, projecting two-storey bays, verandahs, multi-sloped roofs, and tall, decorative chimneys. A mixture of brick and wood is common. Windows often have one large single-paned bottom sash and small panes in the upper sash. Example: 252 James Street South	
Renaissance Revival (1870 - 1910) - Renaissance Revival could be included in the overall term "Italianate". The difference in the styles is that the Renaissance revival is simplified and follows much more closely with the Renaissance proper. The most important aspect of Renaissance design was the search for beauty in the adaptation of simple geometric forms and mathematical principles. It is all about balance. Buildings were planned on a grid that contained circles, squares, and an intricate system of often overlapping geometric shapes. The aim was to create a harmonious design. Example: Sandyford Place (see Page 24)	
Second Empire, 1860-1880 – The mansard roof is the most noteworthy feature of this style and is evidence of the French origins. Projecting central towers and one or two-storey bays can also be present. Example: 46 Herkimer Street